PRAISE FOR

Uncharted Territory

This little book is jam-packed with meaningful stories, wisdom, and sound advice. No matter how many personal-development books you've read, you'll find valuable suggestions here that will further enrich your life. Balance is something we all seek, and Carol Brooks offers a wonderful and readable recipe for attaining it. The starting point is the right attitude, and that's exactly where this enlightening book begins. Read it, highlight it, reread it, and be sure to do the action points. You'll be a better person as a result!

Hal Urban, PhD
Author, *Life's Greatest Lessons* and *Positive Words, Powerful Results*

You-phoria can be elusive, but not for author Carol L. Brooks. In the face of divorced parents, anorexia, and the tragedy of losing a child, she persevered and chose to thrive. You can too! Soak up the lessons in this book, and make them your strategies for success. *Uncharted Territory* will help you find balance and a path to the life you have always dreamed of: you-phoria!

Mark Rieck
CEO, International Right of Way Association, Gardena, California

Self-empowerment through change requires commitment and time. It also requires gaining perspective about ourselves that we are not always best at achieving on our own. In her book *Uncharted Territory*, Carol Brooks unselfishly reveals quite a bit of personal information about her life, her struggles, her weaknesses, and her triumphs. She demonstrates the value of being introspective and honest with oneself about what is not serving one's happiness. But she also offers her readers the tools she has learned through her life that will help them understand themselves better, move forward toward positive change, and, perhaps most importantly, be patient with the process.

Thomas M. Sterner
Author, *The Practicing Mind* and *Fully Engaged*

I've read one hundred plus self-help and motivational books over the years, from Anthony Robbins to Joel Osteen. *Uncharted Territory* tops my list! An easy read and perfect amount of self-help insights to actions, personal stories, and faith. I've already put several of Carol L. Brooks's insights into action, and I look forward to living a purposeful and fulfilled life and becoming the best version of myself.

Mark C. Soehn
Co-founder and principal, Financial Solutions Advisory Group, Inc., Chicago, Illinois

This is a great read. The book is well written, insightful, challenging, transparent and provides a road map for focusing on being positive and living a centered, balanced professional and personal life. Carol Brooks focuses on motivational tools that guide us to pursue being the best we can be. The writer describes how to identify challenging issues in life—burnout, stress, discouragement, and being overwhelmed—and how to take appropriate steps to get back on the path through God-given discipline to become content, fulfilled in life, motivated, balanced, and successful.

Ted Hendrickson
MAI, Hendrickson Appraisal Company, Inc., San Diego, California

No matter what kinds of difficulties you face in life, Carol Brooks's testimonies, lessons learned, encouragement, and challenges will speak to you where you are. Her practical guidance will help you face yourself and your hardship as you grow and overcome.

Peter Lundell
Senior pastor, Walnut Blessings Church, Walnut, California
Author, *Inked for Life* and *Short Stories for the Soul*

Uncharted
TERRITORY

BEING BRAVE ENOUGH
TO EXPLORE ATTITUDES,
HABITS, AND FEARS
TO JOURNEY TOWARD
A BALANCED LIFE

Carol L. Brooks

Published by Cornerstone Management Skills
Escondido, California, USA
www.cornerstonemanagementskills.com

© 2016 by Carol L. Brooks
All rights reserved. Published 2016

Printed in the United States of America
24 23 22 21 20 19 18 17 16   1 2 3 4 5 6
ISBN-13 (trade paper): 978-0-9980556-0-2

Scripture quotations are from the Holy Bible,
New International Version,® NIV,® © 1973, 1978, 1984, 2011 by Biblica, Inc.™
Used by permission. All rights reserved worldwide.

Names have been changed in some of the stories in this book for the sake of privacy.

Cover and interior design by Rob Williams, InsideOutCreativeArts.com

For additional information please visit
www.cornerstonemanagementskills.com,
e-mail cbrooks@cornerstonemanagementskills.com,
or write to P.O. Box 300607, Escondido, CA 92030-0607, USA.

To my mother.

You are my rock.

My shelter.

My strong tower.

My best friend!

Contents

Foreword by Sarita Maybin 13
Preface 17
Acknowledgments 21

1. Right Attitude, Right Solution 23

When Hope Is Swamped by Fear
Attitude 101
Attitude Affects Perspective
Attitude Adjustment: It's a Choice
Think It, Walk It
Harnessing Negative Attitudes

2. Conquering Hurtful Influences of the Past 35

Environment Leads to Attitude Leads to Behavior
Personal-Quality DNA
Releasing Personal-Quality DNA into Each Day
Love Conquers!

3. Change Doesn't Happen Overnight 47

The Exercise of a Lifetime
Step 1: Getting Acquainted with Erikson's Life Stages
Step 2: Identifying the Life Stage Where a Problem Began
Step 3: Committing to Work Through the Struggle
Step 4: Taking the Journey of Self-Assessment
Step 5: Writing Your Story
Step 6: Discovering the Solution to the Problem
Step 7: Processing the Discovery

4. Igniting the Spark Inside You 63

What Triggers Motivation?
Motivation and Reward
Zeroing In on What Motivates You So You Can Help Others
Get Your Passion On

5. Accountability Fuels Your Goals 75

Self-Discipline
Building Self-Discipline
The Enemies of Self-Discipline and How to Squash Them
Personal Accountability Technique
Have Fun!

6. Changing from the Inside Out 87

Change Takes Determination
The Impossible Finish Line
Getting to Work—and Staying with It
Get in the Groove
No Room for Perfectionists
Shout It Out!
Are You Listening?
No Pity Parties, Please!
A Heart of Gratitude
Dwell in Healthy Reality
Nurture Your Mind
Warnings of Self-Sabotage
Become More Patient

7. Breaking the Beast Hidden Deep in a Habit 103

Lifecycle and Strength of a Habit
Defeating a Habit
Make a Plan
Change Your Belief System
Identify the Source of a Habit
Break the Lifecycle of a Habit
Employ Time and Disuse

Echo Your Thoughts
Flip That Thought

8. Reengineering Your Life—Exchanging Bad Habits for Good 119

Reengineering Happens in Seasons
The Space that Habit Once Occupied
Two Attitudes that Make or Break Reengineering Efforts
Start Small
Stay Dependable
Keep Moving Forward
The Happiness Surround
A Scoop of Double-Chocolate Peanut-Butter-Cup Ice Cream, Please!

9. Dealing with Unexpected Change 131

You Have What It Takes to Stand Strong
Tame That Fear
The Sway Factor
Stretch Your Mind
Relinquish Stubbornness
Remove Resistance
Out with the Old, In with the New
Bye-Bye, Comfort Zone

10. Know Yourself, Find Your Purpose 147

Self-Awareness Defined
Finding Your Voice Through Self-Awareness
Actively Search for Your Voice
Actively Listen to Others
Self-Awareness Perspective: Life in Slow Motion
Develop Self-Awareness
Discover What Matters Most
Self-Understanding Plus Self-Acceptance Equals Forgiveness
Be Kind to Yourself
Keep Getting Better

11. Being the Best *You* Possible 161

You're Unique!
What Were You Created For?
No Fair Comparing Yourself to Others
Someone Else May Need What You Have in Your Box
Take an Inventory
Spring Cleaning

12. Keeping a Healthy Frame of Mind 175

Instruction Booklet
Emergency Contact List
Antiseptic Wipes
Gauze Pads and Adhesive Tape
Tweezers
Bandages
Cold Packs
Flashlight and Batteries

13. Avoiding the Occupational Hazard of Burnout 187

Burnout and Its Companion, Stress
Causes of Burnout
Pace Yourself
Create a Family/Fun Bulletin Board
Freshen Up at the End of a Work Day
Listen to Your Body
Stay Alert
Start the Day with a Relaxing Ritual
Set Boundaries
Be Creative
Do Your Favorite Things

14. Guarding Your Life in a World of Demands 199

Manage Your Time
Count All Your Time
Create a To-Do List
Reschedule an Appointment

Keep Your Schedule Under a Microscope
Concentrate on One Thing at a Time
Deal with the Dreaded P Word
Delegate
Manage Your Time by Managing People
Evaluate Your Progress
Create Breathing Space
Cultivate Gratitude
Employ Faith

15. Where Is Your Compass Pointing? 213

Integrity
Fairness
Kill 'em with Kindness
Dignity
Use Your Global Positioning System
Get Your Bearings
Recalculate When Needed

16. Maintaining a Balanced Life 223

Live in the Moment
Live in Gratitude
Live in Integrity
Live in Happiness
Live in Quality
Live in Your Destiny Dream
Live in Fun and Laughter
Live in Twenty-Twenty Vision

Appendix 1: Erik Erikson's Life Stages 235
Appendix 2: Tony Robbins's Concept of Need 237
Appendix 3: Personal Accountability Techniques 239

Create Goal Cards
Review Your Goals Often
Grow Your Character to Reach Your Goals
Build an Accountability Partnership

Compose Affirmation Statements and Tag-Along Sentences
Give Yourself Special Recognition
Create a Memory Bank

Appendix 4: Creating a Mental Map 249
Notes 251

Foreword

By Sarita Maybin

"Motivate me!" That's the flippant comment I've frequently received over the past twenty-plus years when I've shared that I'm a motivational speaker. My response: "People motivate themselves!" Or better yet, "People are motivated to change when the pain of staying the same becomes greater than the pain of changing."

I've discovered, however, that even when people's pain pushes them to the point of wanting change, they may not know *how* to go about changing their lives for the better.

Fortunately, Carol Brooks offers a roadmap in this book for those wishing to move into uncharted territory in their lives. She shares stories and strategies from her own journey as well as from a wide variety of people ranging from Mike Tyson to Tony Robbins. Plus, she provides tangible to-dos on maintaining a positive attitude, building accountability, and affirming the truth about ourselves.

Uncharted Territory sheds light on how to figure out specifically *what* we really mean when we say we want happiness, or what we need when we say we want inner peace, or what we must do if we say we want to pursue our purpose. Then—it tells us *how* to get it!

I especially enjoy three recurring themes in *Uncharted Territory*.

First, *good versus evil*. Carol reminds us of the need to be ever vigilant in "breaking the stronghold of the beast"—that is, bad habits—and replacing them with good habits. She suggests a seven-step strategy, which of course includes accessing accountability partners to keep us on track and rewarding ourselves when we make progress. (A scoop of double-chocolate peanut-butter-cup ice cream, anyone?) As she says, habit becomes a comfort zone. Each time we venture out of our comfort zone, we break the cycle of the habit. Put another way, "Each time you do the replacement deed, you tell the brain that this is the new behavior."

Carol also recommends that we "flip that thought" when it's a negative one and replace it with more considerate self-talk. For example, instead of dwelling on how we've failed in the past, we should recite a positive affirmation like, "A new start to a new me." Or we can take a proverbial page out of Oprah's book and develop a daily practice of writing down five things for which we're grateful.

I love that Carol brings to life the ongoing good-evil/positive-negative dichotomy by reminding us that "it's tough to be depressed and grateful at the same time." Even better is her own realization: "Both loving and carrying around junk in my life could no longer co-exist." Well said!

Second, *patience—change takes time!* "Tolerance." "Endurance." "Staying power." "Persistence." "Fortitude." "Serenity." "No complaints." Carol shares these synonyms of patience to underscore its importance, and she suggests that we choose the word we resonate with, if the word "patience" doesn't do it for us, as a reminder to hang in there!

She provides the perfect patience pep talk: "You messed up. Forgive yourself. Dust yourself off. Move onward!" That's great advice for surmounting setbacks in our day-to-day lives! She aptly sums up the power of patience with this Chinese proverb: "It is better to take many small steps in the right direction than to make a great leap forward only to stumble backward."

And third, *resilience*. Carol encourages us to adopt the "sway factor"—the ability to bend but not break, much like a palm tree, bridge, or skyscraper in a storm. I appreciate her gentle reminder to be flexible and open minded and to go with the flow or, better yet, the idea of stepping back to get a better view of a situation, to "give space" between ourselves and our challenges when we're confused and frightened.

The need to build on the foundation of past experiences is a useful insight that Carol offers in *Uncharted Territory*. She shares her deep disappointment and despair over a teenage son who repeatedly ran away from home, yet each time it happened, she became better prepared to bounce back based on lessons learned the last time. Her lesson: "Not to interpret my failure based upon his choices." We could all benefit from that lesson on so many levels! In the words of Holocaust survivor Viktor Frankl, "When we are no longer able to change a situation, we are challenged to change ourselves."

Indeed, *Uncharted Territory* will provide you with true-north principles to help you live up to your God-given potential—in short, this book will help you *motivate yourself*!

Sarita Maybin
Motivational speaker and communication expert
Author of *If You Can't Say Something Nice, What Do You Say?*

Preface

Inner peace. Happiness. Purpose. Isn't this what we all search for our entire lives? This place of center, of balance, where we can live joyously and be empowered by meaning, fulfillment, and true happiness? This is what I call the you-phoria lifestyle. This amazing experience of joy is the abundant life that God intends every one of us to live.

The problem is, most of us, at one time or other, find ourselves caught in the heartbreak of trial, tragedy, conflict, hurts from the past, or some unwelcome surprise that blindsides us along our path through life. Or we simply get caught in the daily grind of busyness, financial pressure, or excessive demands from those around us. In the difficult times and under the pressures of life, life seems anything but balanced. How do we find the peace, joy, and purpose we so long for?

To find this place of center, we must climb toward it. We must be brave enough to wade into the uncharted territory of our attitudes, past experiences, motivations, habits, desires, and values so that we can see who we really are and work toward lives of balance and purpose.

You see, the major player in a life of you-phoria is *you*!

At a certain point in my own journey, after a youth of much unhappiness and blame casting, I developed a strong sense of responsibility for my own you-phoria—and that led me to a search to regain balance in my unbalanced life. As I started to break down painful barriers from my past, I discovered good news: God wanted to use my past to shape my future. This breakthrough helped build my *you*. My new confident *you*, I discovered, was equipped to take risks, extend my faith, and venture further into uncharted territory.

As my pursuit of you-phoria continued through the years, it became evident to me that I had unknowingly been getting in my own way. Hurt and misunderstanding from my past caused me to repeat old habits over and over. Even after spurts of personal growth, when I should have become more confident in my life's direction, I returned to old habits. Discouraged, I often gave up.

As I pondered inconsistencies in my spurts of you-phoria and my gloomy moments of discontent, compelling questions troubled me: "If God intended for me to live a balanced life, how do I stop this roller-coaster ride of inconsistency?" And, "If God 'keeps us occupied with gladness' (Ecclesiastes 5:20), what is the key to defeating my erratic shifts between contentment and discontentment?"

A word echoed in my mind: "Consistency."

That sounded good. In fact, it sounded like the balance and peace I longed for. But being consistent was easier said than done. How could I navigate toward a life that was consistently in balance? Was this even realistic?

In a word, yes. The climb to realize our dreams, hopes, and aspirations *is* achievable—when we seek after it *consistently* with faith and divine guidance. This is the life that we so long to live—not a life of perfection but of balance and peace and joy.

One of my most significant discoveries as I sought to live consistently was that every unexpected event I had experienced in my life was purposeful and not just happenstance. Understanding this helped me plot my course to an abundant life and live exactly as God intended me, you, and everyone to live. Life became exciting for me when I finally understood that each event, each conversation, each disappointment uncovered the *you* deep within me. This is the *you* that is victorious, more than a conqueror, and willing to exchange life's ashes for beauty.

This *you* resides within each of us.

My journey of facing this vicious cycle and working to free myself from it prompted me to write this book. *Uncharted Territory* provides tools that every person needs in order to stay strong and endure the climb toward a balanced life of fulfillment and happiness. Each chapter pinpoints an area of potentially uncharted territory in our lives and also contains action points to help us evaluate our own lives and address matters that are hindering our journey toward abundant life.

This book also reveals how our travel toward a centered life becomes easier when we let go and let God. If we are patient with ourselves along the way and keep an open mind to the change and growth that God wants to bring about in us, then he, our divine rescue, will ensure that we are never given more than we can handle as we journey through the unexpected situations in our lives toward balanced, joyful lives.

Uncharted Territory is a guidebook to help bring people through the maze of life's experiences. This resource will equip readers to change from the *act* of living to the *art* of living.

Enjoy the travel!

Acknowledgments

Dwell as near as possible to the channel in which your life flows.

HENRY DAVID THOREAU

To my husband, Al, who hung in there when life got really messy and kept our love link strong. Because of your steadfastness, we can now laugh and live in a very large way.

To my children, Carlotta, David, Chris, Casey, and Craig, thank you for teaching me endearing life lessons, those important lessons that only come from real life. I only hope I have taught you as much as you've taught me. By the way, thanks for blessing Dad and me with all those darling cherubs (grandchildren) and for bringing your soul mates into our family. Thank you for completing our family circle.

To my parents, Ruth and William, thanks for a great start in life. Mom, you hung in there with me when others told you not to. Now I can see that God specially chose you to be my mother, because only you could have shown me what unconditional love really means. Dad, you taught me the value of putting forth my best to get the most out of learning. These lessons and patterns of behavior have served me well today.

To my late grandmother, Shige Hamada, God blessed me with a life spring in you. I am eternally grateful for your strength and your encouragement. You are my voice as I make choices toward wholeness. You are my soul's light, a beacon that keeps me focused, determined, and committed to encouraging and strengthening others as you encouraged and strengthened me. You are my gift of inner joy. I praise God that of all the grandchildren you could have been given, he chose me.

To my editor, Becky English, you've become a true partner in grooming this book. Our sessions to collaborate on our ideas have grown into a partnership in which the heart of the author and the expertise of the editor have formed a true alliance. I can't thank you enough for discovering the necessity to climb into the author's heart in order to fully express what the author wants to convey. To Steve Lawson, thank you for your leadership to educate me as my first book becomes a reality.

To Jennifer Cullis, thank you for adding the final proofreading polish to the manuscript. To Carlotta Steffen, I am thankful to you for jumpstarting the original cover design with your keen creative eye and layout. To Rob Williams of InsideOut Creative Arts, I am grateful for your expert creative vision for the book cover and interior layout; you have captured the heart of *Uncharted Territory* in your design. To Jason Chatraw, thank you for converting *Uncharted Territory* into an e-book format and targeting an additional readership.

Finally, yet most importantly, my Lord and Savior, Jesus Christ, you are the divine rescue for the human dilemma. Thank you for walking my path and identifying the potholes and then moving my feet as I blindly trampled along my life path. Your love has no boundaries. Thank you for being the greatest role model in my family's lives.

1

Right Attitude, Right Solution

Attitude is 99 percent conflict management.

Not long ago I met two women at a Parkinson's disease support group that my husband and I were attending due to his ongoing battle with the illness. Despite these two women's similarly challenging experiences, they were enormously different from each other—each woman's outlook was at opposite ends of the mental and emotional spectrum.

Debbie cried through her agonizing account of how her life had changed when her husband became ill. She shared the heart-splintering disappointment of his potentially crippling disease and how the two of them had tried to fix an uncontrollable situation. But fear had planted its destructive seed in her, and her world had become aggravating, discouraging, and exhausting. She no longer recognized herself. She begged for help, but her defensive attitude prevented a breakthrough.

The other woman, Frances, embraced a mantra that had carried her through many dark days: "We may have PD, but PD doesn't have us." She and her husband sometimes laughed at his awkward loss of balance, clumsy coordination, and forgetfulness. They cherished each day, especially the good ones. "Good days grow into memorable events," she told me. "Eventually they offer a small ray of hope."

I then shared with the group my experience, swallowing hard to keep my heart from slamming into my throat, since this was the first time I had spoken openly about my husband's PD. I told of the motto my husband and I had adopted while driving home from his neurologist's office after receiving his own heartbreaking diagnosis of Parkinson's disease. It was the same as Frances's: "We may have this disease, but it doesn't have us."

As I recited my commitment to the group, I sat a bit taller. Together my husband and I could harness the same attitude that Frances had talked about and discover the same rays of hope that kept her in a forward-moving progression.

When Hope Is Swamped by Fear

Unfortunately, the trials we face in life don't always end quickly. I wish I could say that after this meeting I remained an emotional giant, facing every day with strength and resolve. But despite my determination not to let Parkinson's disease control our lives and emotions, my husband's diagnosis, slowing movements, fatigue, acute irritability, confusion, depression, and difficulty feeding himself began to take their toll. My heart broke for him—for us. The catchphrase we had once shared with such gusto began to lose its steam. Fear set in, igniting questions in me about our future: "Will my husband be bedridden? How will I care for him? Am I enough?" These questions entrenched my fear.

Fear is a poison. It magnified my problem and slowly chipped away at my resolve to stay strong. The bigger the fear I faced, the smaller my ability to cope. I had to become fearless, take charge, be brave, and face the issues head on.

Why?

Because my issues were not going away. They might fade for a time, but they would eventually come back—bigger than before. Even though none of us wants it to, sometimes fear grips us and holds us back from stepping out and feeling strong enough to deal with whatever challenges a day may hold. This is why we must learn to face our pain and find solutions in the midst of our trials. This is the path to a life of balance.

Even in my darkest moments, God met me in my pain of fear, depression, angst, and frustration. He offered encouragement, and he poured strength into my weariness. He stood at my side not in judgment but in love. In the depths of my soul, I began to see purpose in my trial as God used it to boost strong character in me. Even though I got in my own way so many times, God was patient with me, as he had been so many times throughout my journey over the years toward a balanced life. He brought me, once again, to a place of hope. And this sense of hope began to open a glimmer of inner strength for my husband as well.

It can do the same for you.

Attitude 101

When life-changing circumstances or deep pain seem to get the better of us, we can sit down and despair, or we can fight back. If we want centered, peaceful, purposeful lives, we need to choose the latter. So how do we take on the trials that have taken us on?

The best way to combat unwelcome difficulties is by changing our attitude. Attitude can promote us, or it can hold us back for years to come. It is that powerful.

Attitude is like a shadow—it follows us wherever we go. If we turn right, it turns right. If we skip, it follows along. But that's where the similarities end, because when we stop, our attitude doesn't always stop. It runs ahead of us, pulling us along. If our attitude is good, then it's no problem to have it out in front. But a bad attitude can grab our hearts and lead us astray.

Attitude, or mind-set, has two powerful outcomes: positive or negative behaviors. Our attitude will either promote us to levels we may never have thought possible, or it will keep us entrapped and helpless. Our challenge is to consistently harness a positive outlook. Keeping the right perspective can determine how we handle conflict.

The mantra my husband and I created at the beginning of his disease, "We may have PD, but it doesn't have us," should have worked, but after a while it was no longer effective for me. Actually, my life was like a revolving door. I'd get rid of one sour attitude, and another one would replace it. For instance, I got rid of fear, but in its place came impatience. Parkinson's disease had slowed down my husband—his thoughts, his speech, his memory—and this meant that *I* had to slow down. Slowing down took patience, which I was in scarce supply of—ugh!

So I created a second motto that was more appropriate to where I was now living life. Whenever a difficult situation arose, I heard in my mind's ear, "A good attitude is the only way to create good solutions." When this thought danced in my mind, I scratched my head, thinking what a pretty package these words made but wondering how this idea could become a reality for me. So I prayed—and prayed some more.

One day, deep in my soul, I heard a simplified version of this second motto: "Right attitude, right solution." I pondered it. I enjoyed its clear and concise message, which let me feel as though this was something I *could* do. I repeated it aloud, again and again. Something new was brewing inside me. This simple affirmation gave me strength. After this, when impatience began to rear its ugly attitude, I recited, "Right attitude, right solution." This new attitude not only helped me stay focused, but it also reinforced our original expression: "We may have PD, but it doesn't have us." Strength began to emerge within me—one affirmation at a time.

Although my husband was on a medication routine, it was anything but routine, since sometimes he forgot to take his medicine. His tremors increased. His thoughts became scrambled. He started speaking in the middle of a sentence. That's when I realized that he was forgetting to take his meds and thus starving his brain of dopamine. Apparently, as can happen with any routine, once he had felt he'd gotten a handle on his meds, he had glided into cruise control.

But that had happened to me too. I hated to admit it, but when I displayed impatience, it was because I'd forgotten my mantras. Yet I got upset with my husband for failing to keep his medication schedule! My bad attitude stifled tolerance and patience.

But out of living miserably, I reclaimed my rallying cry: "Right attitude, right solution." Then, instead of arguing with my husband about taking his meds, I developed a solution for his forgetfulness: I created a meds schedule. Each day he tallied the number of times he took his medication, and this gave him control over his health. The schedule was a smashing success. My new mantra, "Right attitude, right solution," helped me find the right response to this particular challenge.

Attitude Affects Perspective

Attitude can be defined as the direction we lean at any given time. That direction determines our perspective of a situation. Attitude and perspective are close cousins, but the interesting question is, which of them comes first in our lives? Most conflict experts believe that if we have the right attitude, we will keep a right perspective of a problem, which will affect how we react to it.

Having the right attitude helps us see or perceive a problem in a positive and progressive way. For example, my new mantra about Parkinson's disease, "Right attitude, right solution," helped me keep an open mind and create a healthy distance from the problem of my husband not taking his medications. This led to discovering solutions and win-win outcomes. And when life gets tough, win-win outcomes are the ticket to a consistently happy and fulfilled life.

Mind-set plays a huge role in how effective we are in resolving issues and how we react to them. A positive mind-set makes a big difference in helping us keep cool in the heat of conflict. A good attitude can push the black clouds aside and make an opening for rays of hope and promise.

Life is full of surprises—some welcome, others best forgotten. Without warning a storm slams into our lives; one day we feel safe, the next we're devastated. Unfortunately, life doesn't promise us a bed of roses. But we can take charge of negative experiences and perceive those situations through a positive lens.

I'm not talking about seeing life through rose-tinted glasses or trying to find a pie-in-the-sky experience. I'm simply saying that our attitude will determine how we view or perceive a problem. For example, when I brought worry into my husband's disease, I made our rough patches much more difficult than they should have been. I worried about things that might happen in the future—the possibility of his getting Alzheimer's or of eventually being unable to feed himself, swallow, or speak as the debilitating disease attacked his muscles. Fear and worry had me in its grip.

But eventually a third mantra whispered to me, "Why borrow trouble?" If we keep an open mind, we'll find that perspective regarding a problem comes when we need it. My first motto grounded me. The second one kept me strong. This third one kept me focused on the present and not on the future.

Bill Gothard, founder of the Institute in Basic Life Principles, has a great description of worry: "Worry is responsibility God never intended us to have." Behaviors such as worry, angst, and frustration tend to weaken our resolve, and when we entertain them, it's hard for us to receive the emotional and spiritual help we desperately need. If we want a good attitude that leads to a positive perspective, we need to trust God with our situation. He'll take care of the rest. He'll chart our course and bring us victoriously through conflict.

Attitude Adjustment: It's a Choice

No one truly *wants* to nurse a bad attitude, but what is it about us humans that we tend to find comfort in bad attitudes? Yep, we're miserable, but by golly, we'll just wallow in it! This is sad, because misery will deceive us into believing that we don't deserve happiness. When we live in a place of misery, we're steeped in despair; subconsciously we accept our fate and don't look for a way out. What we really need is an attitude adjustment.

Let's face it—we don't do ourselves any favors when we feed the wrong attitude. There's a funny thing about mind-set: the more we practice a certain attitude, the more it becomes ingrained in our behavior, and eventually it becomes second nature. If we feed a bad attitude, it will keep us in emotional cruise control so that we automatically react from a negative disposition.

The good news is that we can reshape our mind-set and make the necessary adjustments to be able to think constructively. We own the power to do unthinkable things when we have the right attitude—this is the simple result of divine intervention in our lives. When we allow God to intervene in our unexpected challenges, we have a limitless resource of grace to change our mind-set from "I'd rather wallow in my unhappiness" to "Little by little I'm changing for the better."

Here's the thing about changing an attitude: it's a choice. Before we can execute change, we need to *choose* change. This is the problem with New Year's resolutions. After the calorie-packed holidays, TV commercials dominate our high-definition screens with the best vitamins, the best diets, the best exercise equipment, but not everyone is mentally ready to choose change on the magical date of January 1. Most people need time to wave good-bye to indulging in holiday shopping, eating large amounts of delicious foods, and other bad habits.

If you've missed the auspicious date of January 1, could today be the right time? Are you ready to choose change?! To choose an attitude adjustment? Are you ready to embark on a journey into uncharted territory in your life and deal with those attitudes that are holding you back?

Consider this simple affirmation to boost your motivation to travel unexplored territory: "Feed the attitude you want to grow; starve the attitude you want to shrink." Set your course, and make a commitment to get better.

Think It, Walk It

What do we do when we want to change our attitude but it just isn't happening? We need to take a look at our thought life.

Thoughts feed attitude. They can promote us or hold us back. That is why we can't afford a single negative thought, because the content of our thoughts will eventually show up in our actions. This is the think-it-walk-it concept. Our actions are continually reinforced by our attitude, and eventually our behavior ends up becoming habit.

Our minds are like computers. We can store ineffective information in them, or we can change our minds by reprogramming our thoughts. But there's one influence we need to watch for: inner dialogue, also known as self-talk. It's the software that programs attitude. It determines how we present ourselves to the world around us. Whatever we put into our mind is reflected in what comes out. The "garbage in, garbage out" concept popular in the late sixties still holds true today. If we allow bad thoughts into our minds, eventually that programming will show up in our behaviors and attitudes.

Even when we are dealing with a particularly big problem, we must not make it bigger by allowing garbage thoughts into our mind. When we allow garbage thoughts, we can quickly forget one of the strongest mantras: "Right attitude, right solution." Garbage thoughts will tell us that there are no right solutions, that there are only entrapment, dissolution, and despair. When we empty our minds of garbage, we have room to fill it with God-sized promises of hope, vision, happiness, and purpose. It leads us to fix our minds on what is true, honorable, right, pure, and worthy of our energy and effort so that we can think about things that are positive and worthwhile.

Harnessing Negative Attitudes

Let's face it—when we are steeped in conflict or tragedy, who among us thinks of what is honorable, right, and pure? Most of us don't. We tend to get confrontational and emotional. Consider a different attitude: we can't control negative thoughts that come to our minds, but we can control what we do with them.

The first thing we must do if we really want to harness our negative attitude is *stop* feeding any negative thoughts we are entertaining. The second thing we must do is replace our negative thoughts by thinking the opposite of what we're feeling in the moment. Opposite behavior will take us 180 degrees from negativity.

If you have a tough time figuring out what an opposite behavior looks like, ask yourself this simple question: "What's the opposite of what I'm feeling right now?" If you're angry, for example, tell yourself that this is an out-of-soul experience and that you need to return to a balanced frame of mind. Then focus on opposite behavior. The opposite of anger is calm. Once you've defined the opposite behavior, tell yourself in a firm voice, "I am returning to my soul. My soul is my protector from the negative behavior that brings angst, frustration, and despair into my life. This is where joyous living blossoms. This is where I'm meant to flourish."

Conclusion

Be encouraged today. If you are mired in trouble or heartache or frustration, you can reprogram your thoughts and create acceptable behaviors. Grasp the right perspective of whatever problem you are facing, and take the necessary steps to keep fear, worry, or doubt from knocking you off center.

And remember, you are human. Don't be hard on yourself. As you begin to take authority over your attitudes and thoughts, take an assessment of your progress at points along the way, and realize that, little by little, you're getting better. Don't forget to recite, "Right attitude, right solution." Take a deep breath, and invite God to illuminate your journey.

Learn, as I have learned, to cherish these powerful mantras:

1. We may have PD, but PD doesn't have us.
2. Right attitude, right solution.
3. Don't borrow trouble.

Each is unique, but all of them have helped me help my husband. I recall the wedding vows I blindly recited forty-three years ago as a so-in-love bride that nothing else mattered: "For better or for worse, in sickness and in health." Through all these years, God has met my husband and me where we have lived life. He has always been with us, giving us the mind-set we have needed to run our race. The truth is, he'll do the same for you.

Action Points

A critical assessment of your attitude and the consequence of it is instrumental in devising a plan to change from a negative to a positive mind-set. Take a few minutes to think about each question, and then document your thoughts.

What would you say to your teenage self that had a haughty attitude?

Write down an experience that has caused a change in your attitude.

What victory stories can you share about the benefits of feeding the right attitude and starving a bad one?

Do you tend to repeat the same behavior? If so, what attitude supports that behavior? Give the attitude a name, and make a commitment to fix it.

2

Conquering Hurtful Influences of the Past

We are where we are, as we are, because of what we are.

EARLE J. GLADE

My suitcase bulged with clothes, shoes, a large cosmetic bag, and my all-important tubes of lipstick that matched every outfit. As I rolled the suitcase up to the ticketing counter at the airport, I feared that I might have exceeded the weight limit on my luggage. I wished I hadn't packed so much stuff!

Isn't that how our attitudes sometimes become—"over packed" by the influences around us? This is just one of many burdens that can bog us down on our journey toward a balanced life. Our minds can become weighed down with negative and hurtful words that people say to us. Eventually we form our own ideas of how we think of ourselves, but if we judge ourselves by someone else's measuring stick, the perception we develop of ourselves can cause us to become our own worst critics.

When this happens, we become people who second-guess ourselves. We are quick to ask ourselves, "What was I thinking?" especially when we've made a poor decision. If we lived by "hindsight is twenty-twenty," many of our "What was I thinking" disappointments could be avoided. But in real life we berate ourselves with this and other perplexing questions: Why do I think more bad thoughts than good about myself? Why do I think bad thoughts about others? Why do some people make it big while I struggle?

These probing questions shape our attitudes and behaviors because they have been fueled by our environment. We wonder how some people come out of horrible life experiences with positive attitudes while others fall victim to similar events; but the influences people were raised with have shaped their attitudes, and attitude affects behavior. That's the reason some people can hold on to a positive attitude regardless of their situation: they were brought up in a positive environment. If our environment, on the other hand, says it's okay to live half empty, then we tend to fall into the emotional trappings of feeling that we don't measure up.

If we want to live lives that are free of burdens and emotionally and mentally balanced, we need to understand a prominent factor in our lives: human behavior.

Environment Leads to Attitude Leads to Behavior

During a psychology class I took in my freshman year in college, the professor asked us to write an essay answering the question "Who am I?" Thankfully he had given us two weeks to complete the assignment, because I was still struggling with the definition of who I was the night before the paper was due. I finally decided to write about the different roles I had played in my life: a daughter, a granddaughter, a stepdaughter, a girl dating someone her parents didn't approve of. This assignment helped me define who I was at seventeen and who I wanted to become as an adult.

As I wrote, I began to reconsider what I had thought to be my parents' ridiculous house rules: be home at midnight, don't smoke or do dope or hang around people who do, study hard, get good grades, be an upstanding citizen, go to church, mind your manners. I also thought about their dislike of my boyfriend. As I judged who I now was against their standards, I began to understand that my parents' over-protectiveness was an indication that they had nurtured my success, not destroyed my happiness.

The first commitment I made after writing the essay was to break up with my boyfriend. Deep inside I knew he wouldn't be good for me in the long run. I cried for several days over losing him, because a part of me really cared for him, but a few years later I saw more clearly the wrong path I could have taken with him.

The most important lesson I learned in my first year in college is that behavior is shaped through environment—and my family environment of my parents sticking their noses into my business made me want to rebel wherever and whenever I could. But I also learned that I could reshape myself by defining who I wanted to become.

As I embarked upon this journey of change, the influences and voices from my family and from teachers in my past needed to be quieted. This required a huge effort on my part.

All of us could come up with a long list of names that people have called us. Although we may have heard these names years ago, they may still chime in our minds today. As a young adult, I struggled to carve my own trail, to shape my identity without my parents' watchful eye on me. I wanted my independence; I needed my independence. But accusations that had been leveled against me by various adults in my life seemed to block my path—"lazy," "unmotivated," "barely getting by"—and soon I began to think that I wasn't smart enough to accomplish an independent lifestyle.

Our behaviors and attitudes are shaped by the voices we've heard since childhood. These influences come from parents, relatives, teachers, friends—anyone who has swayed us with their worldviews. When we are children, we store people's persuasive beliefs in our minds, and these beliefs eventually have an effect on how we develop as an adult. Some words and opinions from our past we tend to focus on, while others we choose to neglect. That is why we blossom in some areas and are weak in others. If we were raised in a loving home, we can expect to give and receive love; we've been preconditioned to this behavior because things like love, consideration, and forgiveness were given to us. The way we were treated as children is recorded in our minds, and when we grow up, it shapes how we perceive our world.

When we cram our minds with negative life experiences the way some of us over-pack a suitcase, it's no wonder we become bogged down with unhappiness and heartache. We always have a choice of what attitudes to keep in our suitcase; the tough part is choosing wisely.

Personal-Quality DNA

As adults, we have the freedom to either harbor negative childhood impressions or ignore them. The choice becomes easier to make, however, when we utilize what I like to call "personal-quality DNA"—the qualities that we all naturally possess in varying degrees: integrity, love, compassion, patience, joy, kindness, goodness, gentleness, self-control, motivation, sound reasoning, and peace. These traits are etched into our hearts by God, and when we apply them to our lives, they become divine instincts that empower right thinking, right behavior, and right choices.

Personal-quality DNA is a powerful magnet that pulls us toward success. If we're frustrated by negative thoughts and find that we are spinning our wheels, we must step outside the spin and get into our authentic makeup. Standing firm upon the DNA God built into us ultimately causes us to seek those choices that result in harmony and stability. When we exercise personal-quality DNA, we make choices that draw us toward our place of center—toward a balanced and satisfied life. When we live in center, we live in total authenticity. But when we shift off center and become imbalanced, less favorable traits surface: jealousy, anger, depression, frustration, blame.

A particular TV cartoon intrigued me as a child. In the story a character was faced with a challenge. It was up to him to make a choice to do right or wrong, but he didn't know what to do. Instantly a smaller version of himself hopped onto his shoulder in the form of an angel with wings. On his other shoulder stood the devil, wearing a red cap with horns and holding a pitchfork. Excitement brewed when the angel and devil argued about a solution to the character's challenge. The character's mind was overwhelmed by the persuasive voices of the angel and the devil. The character jerked his head from side to side as he listened intently to the voices of his conscience. As I watched, I tried to put myself in the place of the character, wondering what I would do. Whose voice would I listen to? In the end, truth and goodness prevailed, and the character lived happily ever after.

As adults, we're faced with the same choices of right or wrong—to live within our personal-quality DNA or not. The ability to do the right thing has been ingrained in us from our childhood. So why do we burden ourselves with sour attitudes? Why don't we consistently choose to repack our minds with thoughts that move our lives forward? Each of us has been created with a God-shaped character makeup. When we operate in our personal-quality DNA of love, honesty, compassion, patience, joy, kindness, goodness, gentleness, we live at our highest potential. If we live in honesty, we'll be successful. If we live in joy, we'll be happy. Life will be good. All will be well.

Releasing Personal-Quality DNA into Each Day

Unfortunately, our lives don't always run like fine-tuned machines. We have our ups and downs, and it's the down times that test our attitude. But if we want to behave in our personal-quality DNA, we're better able to do so when we recognize how much our past influences our present and contributes to the character traits that we exhibit.

We are better able to solve a problem if we are willing to understand our past and identify attitudes that prevent us from moving forward. This is what Sonja tried to do. Although emotionally exhausted after years of working for a verbally abusive boss, fear of upsetting him and possibly getting fired caused her to keep silent. One day, however, when her boss unleashed his anger, she'd had it. She recalled a conversation that she and I had held about unresolved childhood issues that were carried into adulthood, and she began to search her childhood for events that may have caused her awkward boss-employee relationship.

She identified her mother as a source of tormenting verbal abuse. Sonja recalled never measuring up to her mother's high expectations. Beaten down, Sonja had silently tolerated the abuse. She now understood that low self-esteem had followed her into adulthood. But before she was able to speak to her boss, her past had to be addressed.

She called her mother, who immediately began berating her for not visiting often. As usual, her mother started with one problem and then dug up other mistakes from Sonja's past. Taking a deep breath, Sonja interrupted. "I know you love me, Mom, but you don't demonstrate your love by the hurtful things you say." After a few seconds of silence, her mother explained how much she loved her and wanted only the best for her. Sonja bravely told her mom that offering support would be the only form of love she could accept. Together they made a commitment to stop the tango of verbal abuse and restore their relationship by loving each other. Love is one of the components of personal-quality DNA.

Once Sonja had dealt with her past, she was able to say, "I am no longer that intimidated little girl. I will not carry that baggage into my adult life." Low self-esteem and fear no longer belonged in her suitcase. Now she was ready to confront her boss. This time she drew integrity from her personal-quality DNA. With honesty, Sonja told her boss how badly his distrust made her feel. He apologized to her, promising to treat her with the same respect she had always shown him.

Love Conquers!

So how do we live increasingly in our personal-quality DNA and overcome hurtful influences of our pasts?

Think back to when you were a child and did your chores neatly and on time. What happened? You were probably rewarded, and because of that, your self-esteem blossomed. Your good behavior was reinforced, and you looked forward to repeating good behavior, because the reward was worth the effort and it reinforced your motivation to do the right thing. Since you had done the right thing, you were happier with yourself. Confidence became a strength in your life, and every time you continued to do the right thing, confidence grew, and your affection for yourself grew.

This is the key to finding victory over the hurtful things people have said to us and to living balanced, healthy lives. When we're able to love ourselves, we become alert to how we live and how we're being treated. That's what Sonja did. She became fed up with sitting in the bull's-eye of her boss's anger. She put her foot down one day and said, "No more!" She loved herself enough to make a commitment to change—to step into uncharted territory that would lead to improving her self-esteem. Love conquered it all for Sonja, and it can do the same for you.

But sometimes we can get in our own way. When we choose not to live in our personal-quality DNA, guilt comes knocking on our doors. As a result, we do not feel good about ourselves. Guilt screams at us, reminding us that we messed up, that we're less than, that we never do anything right. We speak to ourselves in demeaning tones. If we're not careful, we can allow our heavy hearts to lead us into other negative situations. Because we're not happy with ourselves, we push away love and invite hatred to affect the way we feel about ourselves. But only we have the motivation to change our dilemmas. Real living happens when we love ourselves enough to say, "I deserve to live happily. I deserve to exercise personal-quality DNA. I deserve to live as victoriously as God has planned for me to live." And because this is God's plan, he'll guide us through our journeys—triumphantly!

Throughout life we've all had opportunities to recognize that true authenticity and happiness come from growing positive character attributes in our personal-quality DNA. Sure, we may have to travel through the uncharted territory of our past trials and difficulties, but that's when we realize that our life experiences can shape and strengthen our DNA. The confidence we gain from having a strong DNA will open our eyes to opportunities for future success and fulfillment. Then, once we've had a taste of living with purpose, we'll be willing to change any attitude or behavior that jeopardizes living at our full potential.

Wouldn't it be great if we could kick back and automatically live to our full potential? The reality is that living in the fullness of who we are and are meant to become means effort on our part. There isn't an easy road to happiness. There isn't an elevator that will take us swiftly to success either. We need to focus on separating ourselves from negative and critical attitudes that cause us to live beneath our full potential. If we don't have confidence within ourselves to live our best lives, then it will be easy for us to give up or not start at all. "Why bother?" is an attitude we pack in our minds. At the core of the "Why bother?" attitude is the fear of failure. Our attitude tells us not to put effort into strengthening our personal-quality DNA because we'll probably fail anyway. But we can quiet the voice of fear when we love ourselves unconditionally.

Love is foundational to how we see ourselves, how we judge ourselves, and how we develop attitudes about ourselves. Whenever I begin to think negative thoughts about myself, I quickly ask, "Where is unconditional love?" If we allow true love to work on our behalf, then no room remains for negative thoughts, because love is like a vacuum cleaner—it sucks up any thoughts or attitudes that don't work in our favor. Love will suck up fear that cripples our confidence. Love will pave the way for us to full lives with words of encouragement. When we live in love, then all our thoughts and behaviors are orderly, controlled, and balanced. We actualize our personal-quality DNA and live the way we were meant to: richly, happily, and successfully. When we love ourselves unconditionally, we're able to pass that love on to others.

Have you considered the breadth of God's unconditional love? His love is immeasurable; actually, there are no boundaries to his love. His love is the kind that says, "I don't care how many times you mess up, I still love you." We could mess up fifty times in one day and go to God fifty times, and he would forgive us each time. The outpouring of his love isn't contingent upon a calculator that adds up our transgressions. When we come to him for forgiveness, he promises to forgive us, and as far as the east is from the west, he'll cast our missteps and remember them *no more* (see Psalm 103:12). Further in this psalm, in verse 17, David, the psalmist, declares, "From everlasting to everlasting the LORD's love is with those who fear him." I scratch my head at that, thinking about the enormity of "everlasting to everlasting"—that's got to be forever.

If God loves us unconditionally, then why don't we love ourselves unconditionally? When we don't love ourselves the way we should and we complain that we're less than, we're telling an almighty God—who loves us unconditionally—that he made us less than, and if he made us less than, then he must have made everything junk.

Conclusion

The next time you ask, "What was I thinking?" check in with yourself. Assess your behavior, and identify the attitude and the influence from the past that may be holding you back. Now identify one of the qualities of your personal-quality DNA that will bring you back to your true self, and claim the power of who you are.

Don't forget to inspect your suitcase from time to time. Throw out all the stuff that bogs you down, and once you have some extra room, be sure to fill the suitcase with your personal-quality DNA. Toss out jealousy, anger, depression, frustration, and blame from your suitcase, and fill it with integrity, love, compassion, patience, joy, kindness, goodness, gentleness, self-control, motivation, sound reasoning, and peace.

You owe it to yourself to travel with a suitcase packed with all the strengths embodied in your personal-quality DNA. Only then will you continue to move forward to a balanced, peaceful, and purposeful life. When life gets in the way and you lose your focus, remember to love yourself, and watch how other elements of personal-quality DNA will rally to your side: forgiveness, patience, kindness—all products of unconditional love. Loving yourself means accepting yourself just as you are.

Loving yourself also means understanding that God wants to complete a good work within you. He will never give up on you. You shouldn't give up on yourself. Set your sails with the winds of unconditional love, and enjoy your journey.

Action Points

Our minds are like computers. We tend to store advice and comments from others. Some comments are hurtful and should be deleted from our minds, while positive comments should be kept. Make a list of positive thoughts you should keep.

An important step to identifying your attitudes is giving them a name: angry, negative, defensive, etc. Let's say you were recently engaged in a confrontation; what name would you give your attitude?

If the name you gave your attitude was negative, how would you change it to a positive one?

Take some time to answer the question "Who am I?"

3

Change Doesn't Happen Overnight

There is in every child, at every stage, a new miracle of vigorous unfolding, which constitutes a new hope and a new responsibility for all.

ERIK ERIKSON

The night before my seventh birthday I had a prayer request. I had learned at school that day that if we had faith, we could ask for anything, and poof, we'd get it. So at bedtime I closed my eyes tightly, folded my hands, and asked God to give me a horse for my birthday. I told God that when I grew up I wanted to be a cowgirl and that every cowgirl needed a horse. I mustered as much faith as I could drum up in my almost-seven-year-old heart and prayed hard. As I dozed off to sleep, I envisioned tying up my horse at the rickety old fence in the grassy common area behind our urban apartment complex.

The next morning I peeked out the bedroom window, my heart ready to burst with excitement, and scanned every inch of the backyard.

No horse. I was devastated.

Wouldn't life be grand if we awoke one morning to find that, in place of all our insecurities and bad habits, we were filled with strength, certainty, and peace? Although we're not seven-year-old children wanting something without considering the consequences, yet a child resides within each of us and wishes for more confidence, happiness, and courage. At some time in our life's journeys, many of us have prayed for these attributes, mustered up strong faith, and expected God to magically answer our prayers *right now*, only to awaken with absolutely none of the changes we prayed for. "Come on!" we've pleaded. "If anyone could answer this prayer with a poof, it would be you, God."

But things like confidence, happiness, and courage don't just happen. We must climb the mountain toward abundant life, and as we do, what *does* happen is that we develop a hunger to improve the quality of our lives and grow from our past experiences.

The Exercise of a Lifetime

According to Erik Erikson, developmental psychologist and psychoanalyst, our behavioral development is shaped by life events that take place at various stages throughout our lives. Erikson has organized life into eight stages from birth to death (see appendix 1). Each stage of development can affect our success or failure in our quest for balanced lives.

Some time ago I developed an exercise using Erikson's life stages to assist people who, like myself, are interested in venturing into uncharted territory in their lives. The purpose of the exercise is to reflect upon the various stages of our lives and pinpoint the roots of issues that we hope to see changed. As we discover the sources of our insecurities, fears, and negative habits, we will be able to address those matters and be freed from our bondage to them.

When I first did this exercise, it awakened me to negative attitudes I needed to overcome. This exercise helped me break through barriers I had unknowingly lugged around all my life. It also helped me identify emotional pain and give it a name. For example, as I remembered someone leaving me, this exercise enabled me to give my pain a name: loss. This enabled me to stop blaming the person who had left me and objectively focus on overcoming my loss.

The result of doing this exercise was invaluable to me. Through this process of self-assessment that I completed over time, I was set emotionally free from offenses that I had once given permission to follow, plague, and confuse me. As I share my own journey through Erikson's life stages, which I call my "exercise of a lifetime," look for the benefits of this exercise and see how it may apply to your own circumstances.

Step 1: Getting Acquainted with Erikson's Life Stages

There are several facets to Erikson's life stages. At each life stage, Erikson states, a person must deal with a particular crisis, or conflict; if this crisis is successfully navigated, it will lead to a certain outcome, or virtue. To get started on my "exercise of a lifetime," I read through Erikson's table to acquaint myself with his analysis of each life stage.

After familiarizing myself with Erikson's chart, I carefully matched my life events to each stage. I made mental notes of how my experiences fit into his table. If you plan to match your own experiences to these stages, I suggest limited note taking as you orient yourself with Erikson's philosophy, as it can bog you down and become a form of self-analysis. It's more important at first simply to get a general understanding of Erikson's stages and the stages of your own life that you want to focus upon.

Step 2: Identifying the Life Stage Where a Problem Began

Once comfortable with Erikson, I zeroed in on a stage in my life in which I had felt the most pain and disappointment. I felt a surge of emotional pain when I read the explanation of Erikson's fourth life stage—school age (six to twelve years): "If we experience unresolved feelings of inadequacy and inferiority . . . , we can have serious problems in terms of competence and self-esteem."[1] This was my starting point.

Once I had identified where my pain began, I tried to give my pain a name. I had to think about cause and effect, starting at ground zero and following the path from the beginning of my pain and disappointment. Eventually a name rose up for me: unhappiness. As I pondered, I realized that the pain of unhappiness I had felt as a child had repeated itself throughout my life.

Now I was ready to embark upon the path from childhood to where I was now.

Step 3: Committing to Work Through the Struggle

I made a commitment to stay open and honest as I embarked upon this journey. Not knowing what to expect, I asked God for guidance and for help to be patient with myself while facing the source of certain issues in my life. It was important that I arrive on the other side of my anguish—that I be brave enough to want change more than to avoid pain.

Being committed to honesty helped me learn more about who I really was today—why I reacted the way I did and said the things I said. The truth of my unhappiness was revealed as I peeled off layers I had added throughout my life—layers I had hoped would protect me from the pain. As I faced my pain openly, I was able to assess the cause of my unhappiness—and I discovered that I had unknowingly been focused on the wrong culprit.

Step 4: Taking the Journey of Self-Assessment

Self-assessment is a process. As I sought answers to my unhappiness over the next days and weeks, certain thoughts followed me like a shadow throughout each day. These thoughts weren't burdensome or annoying; rather I just wondered about them. For example, what event had *first* caused my unhappiness?

As I searched, the first unhappy event was revealed, then the next, and so on. Taking this journey was like uncluttering an overpacked suitcase, one item at a time. For me this was a profound path toward cleansing and completeness.

Step 5: Writing Your Story

When I had accumulated enough understanding of my pain, it was as though cataracts were peeled away from my hindsight. Now I was ready to write my story. Bravely I began to travel into uncharted territory, where the answers were waiting for me.

Although I knew I had suffered with feelings of being "not enough" for most of my childhood, after reading Erikson's life stages, I began to see that I had actually been a very unhappy child. This revelation came as a bit of a shock, because I had always been a positive thinker, even as a child, and had always looked for the glass half full. I had known as a little girl that something was wrong inside me, but I now saw that I had shoved my struggles down deep inside and instead played hard, laughed hard, and greeted each day with new opportunities for fun and surprise. Now I was face to face with my inner challenges.

So why the unhappiness? To help me understand its cause, I tried to think of a time when I had been happy and then determine what might have changed in my young life. As I searched the past, I eventually remembered being truly happy when I was living in Hawaii (where I had been born) with my mom and my grandmother, Babasan. Home life was secure, carefree. I knew I was loved. We enjoyed picnics with family and friends at the beach. I played outside in the rain. Our home was filled with delicious island foods and soothing Polynesian music, and a comfortable and colorful sack dress called a muumuu was the daily attire. But one day my little world changed.

When I was five, my mom, Babasan, and I moved to the mainland. I didn't like the food—hamburgers, hot dogs, pizza, soda. Where were the rice, seaweed, barbecued chicken, and potato salad with tuna and peas and shredded carrots? The people were different too—blonde, fair-skinned, with blue eyes and long, straight noses. They spoke with an accent. I missed my family and playmates back home.

My teacher embarrassed me at school. She said I didn't speak proper English. She'd say that no one could "shut" or "open" the light. "You shut or open a window," she told me. Nor could I describe something as "da kine." Instead of saying generally, "It was da kine dress," I should say, "It was a pretty dress or a long dress or a short dress." I was humiliated in front of my classmates.

Who cared about the details of a dumb dress! What was wrong with these people? Maybe nothing was wrong with them. Maybe everything was wrong with me.

By age seven I began to gain weight. I had been a thin little girl in Hawaii. Now I wondered, was my weight gain due to unhappiness after being uprooted from my secure home?

My biggest problem, however, was that I didn't think my mom loved me anymore, since she had forced me to leave my family, friends, and toys at home in Hawaii. I'd had a cardboard box as large as me that had held my entire family of baby dolls—but I could only take one. I loved all my dolls; the ones left behind wouldn't have a mommy. I felt anxious and cried as I stood by the box.

Mom promised to buy me more baby dolls when we got to the mainland, but I didn't want new babies. I begged her to leave me behind, but she said she was moving me to the mainland for a better life and that vast opportunities for education, career, and marriage would satisfy my every dream. Of course she did want all my dreams to come true, but I just felt she was mean.

My mom was a beautiful Japanese woman with skin the richness of chocolate, a petite figure, and long black hair that danced in the wind. Men hung out their car windows as they drove by her, whistling as she walked down the street. It was no surprise that she began dating as soon as our feet touched the shores of San Diego. In a way it made me happy because the attention made her happy.

One day Mom brought home a man I didn't like. His laughter sounded fake. He laughed at things that weren't funny. He didn't look at people when he spoke. He was a small-framed Japanese man, nothing like my real daddy, who was tall and handsome and had a big smile.

I blamed my mom that I didn't have my real daddy. She had left him when I was six months old; she said he had beaten her. But he was kind to me. My daddy was Portuguese, standing six-five with thick black hair like Carey Grant's. Daddy made me feel special. I didn't see him much, but when he did visit from his nearby Air Force base in Modesto, he let me sit on his lap, and I'd press my hand into his palm. His hands were gigantic, and I felt protected and loved. He smelled good too; Mom said it was his aftershave. Daddy let me sit in the front seat of his car, and he'd hold my hand as we walked the sidewalks of San Diego. He loved chocolate ice cream, just like I did. He called me his princess.

My mom's new boyfriend, however, made snide remarks to me. Tears filled my eyes as he teased me about my weight. "Must be jelly, 'cause jam don't shake like that," he'd say, or, "There goes the tub of lard." He was mean—and to me that made my mommy mean for being with him.

My mom's boyfriend and I fought continually. I said mean things to him, and my mom warned me that I'd be punished. I didn't care—that is, until she dragged me to the bathroom and washed my mouth out with soap. I sobbed and gagged with her long fingers down my throat. Why didn't she wash his mouth out with soap when he called me a tub of lard? Instead she slapped my face and said that children should be seen and not heard.

Babasan was the rock in my life. She was a loving disciplinarian, acting as both mother and father to me. We'd lie in bed at night with all the lights out, and she'd tell me *obake* (ghost) stories. I'd cling to her side, sure that an *obake* was somewhere in our apartment. She was a fun playmate too. She sewed small and colorful bags filled with tiny beans, and we played toss and catch. But most of the time we played house with my new baby dolls. Yes, Mom had kept her promise, and I loved my new dolls, but I was still sad, wondering who was loving all the babies I had left behind.

I knew that God was important, because Babasan prayed all the time to Buddha at the *Hotokesan* (shrine) in the bedroom that she and I shared. She offered rice and fresh fruit to him and to her beloved deceased. I stood close to her side as she chanted prayers and bowed repeatedly in front of the *Hotokesan*. With eyes shut, head bowed, hands folded in prayer, and a ring of beads draped over her thumbs, she was my shelter, my strong tower. Within her shadow I felt safe.

When my mom announced her upcoming wedding to her boyfriend, I sat on the front porch, crying. I was nine. I begged my mom not to marry him, to remarry my real daddy instead, but she said her boyfriend had a good-paying job and could give us a good life—I could go to college, have a big wedding. But who cares about college or a big wedding at nine? I only wanted my mommy to want me, but she chose somebody else.

When my mom remarried, my stepdad didn't want Babasan to live with us. Babasan had always been with me. I was scared to be without her. I pled for my mom to kick my stepdad out and let Babasan share my bedroom as we'd always done. But Mom said she couldn't. I knew why. She loved him more than me. I wrung my chubby hands, frightened. Mom did it again—she chose her new husband over me.

But one day the ugly storm began to change the direction of its surge.

After my mom was married, whenever my stepdad and I fought, my mom began to rise up like a fierce lioness protecting her cub. When that happened, I felt loved. Still, if she hadn't married him in the first place, I wouldn't have been so unhappy. Despite some softening in my heart toward my mom, I still blamed her for my misery.

I gained more weight after my mom remarried. Kids teased me and called me names. But my mom never did. She sewed pretty dresses for me and said how nice I looked. She pinned satin ribbons in my hair to match my outfits.

Over the next few years Mom started to spend more time with me. Her encouragement and support slowly changed my attitude. I became more confident. But unhappiness still plagued me. The only time my parents communicated was in arguments over how badly my stepdad taunted me, since in his eyes I never measured up.

But then I didn't care what he thought. I was a teenager now, and he still laughed at things that weren't funny, still wouldn't look at people when he spoke with them. If I was ever going to be happy, I had to get out of this house.

Mom was particular about who I dated. He had to be white, she said. "That's the only way you'll get ahead in this world," she told me. I didn't care if the guy was purple; I just needed out of the house. At eighteen and during my first semester in college, my white high-school boyfriend and I married.

I didn't have that big wedding my mom had boasted about when I was nine. I didn't have a wedding dress. No flowers. No bridal party. No wedding shower. No invitations or professional photographer. Instead Bob and I married in a pastor's office. I wore a beige wide wale corduroy suit that my mom had sewn for me. But it didn't matter; this was my ticket out. Now I could make my own happiness.

Bob and I *were* happy—at first. We both went to school, and he worked nights. Bob was outgoing, and our apartment was a constant hangout for his friends. I didn't like the empty beer bottles all over the place or the guys who were too drunk to hit the toilet when they used it. But we were happy. Especially when our daughter was born. Bob was so proud of her; he and I played with her for hours.

But little by little the tension of our new responsibility became a fissure in our relationship.

Still, we worked hard to stay together. My mom, however, wasn't so helpful when it came to my marriage. Now that I had my daughter, Mom started visiting a lot, unannounced of course. She waltzed through the apartment, telling me all the things I was doing wrong as a wife and mother. Mom always said she had my best in mind, so I listened to all her instructions. But that's when my marriage tattered at the edges—and nothing could hold it together.

Bob and I began to fight constantly. I breathed down his throat the same way my mom did mine. He could do nothing right. My mom said I should leave him, and she offered to pay for a divorce attorney. One day she and I sat in her attorney friend's office, where she proudly told him how satisfied she was with herself for breaking up my marriage. It hadn't been destined to last anyway, she said, so she had quickened the inevitable.

Mom had ripped me away from Hawaii. She hadn't let Babasan live with us after she got remarried. She hadn't given me a big wedding. Now she had broken up my marriage. Never mind the fact that she had stood up for me to my stepdad after she remarried. I had every reason to blame her for *everything*.

I was frightened to live on my own and raise my daughter and the second child I was now carrying. How would I raise two babies? I could barely care for myself.

Mom wanted me to move back home, but most frighteningly, she wanted to adopt her grandchildren. "Go see the world," she said. "Finish college. Make something of yourself. Have fun."

But I could never let anyone raise my children, even though I was only eighteen and frightened out of my mind. I rejected Mom's offers.

But it turned out that I wasn't alone in raising my daughter and making the trek to doctor exams and attending college—Mom was there for us. She bought bags of groceries, baby clothes, diapers, laundry soap. Thanks to my mother, we lacked for nothing. Sure, my mom nagged, but I began to realize that it was incidental in exchange for all her support. My attitude toward my mother began to soften, even though, thanks to her, I was now divorced.

I went into labor during my eighth month of pregnancy. After a short physical exam, the doctor couldn't find my baby's heartbeat.

My baby was dead, he told me in an icy tone.

During the dark hours of that night, my mother stood at my bedside. My mom, who never showed any sign of emotion, now looked at me through eyes filled with sorrow. No words were exchanged between my mother and me in that dimly lit labor room, but I grabbed her hand and held on to her like an anchor for the first time I could remember.

How does a mother exist after the death of her child? I slowly ran my hand over my flattened stomach that, just a few days before, had been round and resting on my lap. But now my womb was empty. My arms were empty. My heart was empty.

My mother nursed me back to health for weeks and slowly helped me accept my new reality. She cared for me and her granddaughter twenty-four seven. When my mind was scattered, she became my direction. My rock. My shelter. My strong tower.

As I relived the details of my story and traced the path of my unhappiness, I finally understood that my unhappiness wasn't my mother's fault. Her marriage to a wealthy man who had met our every need and unlimited wants turned out exactly as she had said it would be: he had taken care of us.

Eventually God healed my relationship with my stepdad too. As my attitude began to change, I realized that he seemed kinder than I had always thought. Through this different lens, I saw that he was keenly interested in my success. I had worked hard in my youth to create a fissure in my parents' relationship; I had desperately hoped that my mom would divorce my stepdad or that he would leave. But he never left—he never abandoned me.

I began to see that of all the dads God could have given me, he had given me the best. My stepdad had given up evenings after hard days at work to help me with homework. He had taught me to be persistent in learning. I hadn't appreciated it at the time, but he had made me do "neat work." No sloppy erasing. "Be proud of your work," he had told me. He had shown me that hard work pays off. Now, as I wrote my story, I was able to see that during all the nights I had cried myself to sleep, wanting a daddy who loved me, he and I had shared the same roof.

Step 6: Discovering the Solution to the Problem

When I finished my story and the self-analysis that went along with it, I made a discovery that connected all the broken pieces in my life and eventually guided me to wholeness: when my unhappiness was honestly addressed, I didn't have to hold on to it anymore.

Once I was able to release the pain, I found that I was able to weave my way through misunderstanding, confusion, disappointment, and loss. This led to clarity and eventually to healing and peace.

Step 7: Processing the Discovery

The last step in this process was making a gathering place to collect all my thoughts and conclusions from steps 1 through 6.

What had been the cause of all my unhappiness? Of all my feelings of being unloved, unwanted, undesirable? It wasn't my mother. It had all started when I was five years old, when we moved from Hawaii. Everything in my life had become difficult at that point, and I had held on to the past and allowed unhappiness to taint my perception of reality.

Over the years I had directed all my ammo at the very person who only wanted the very best for me. The good qualities I have and the person I am today are because when God searched the world for my caregiver, my supporter, and eventually my best friend, he chose my mother. Through my restoration I fell in love with her all over again.

I can't begin to say how liberated I have been since discovering the root cause of my unhappiness. It uncluttered my heart and helped me get rid of the naysayers from my childhood, comments from people I had looked up to—my parents, my aunt and uncle, teachers. Some of their taunting labels had been "You're sloppy," "stupid," "shiftless." I was now brave enough to detach from and toss out these ugly voices and attitudes that had kept me stagnant and entrapped. This cleared the dark clouds of unhappiness from my life, and I became able to recognize and appreciate the advocates in my life—people who had tried to convince me that my mother loved me. I had tried to believe them, but it wasn't until I could feel her love with my heart that I understood, truly understood, how deeply she cared for me. Now I hold on to positive truths about myself. Doing this created stepping-stones to building character and eventually happiness in my life.

Once the cataracts of blame were gone, I could clearly see that I had never been alone on my journey. Not when I despised my mother or was angry when she remarried or cried myself to sleep because it was the only time I could be alone without my mom barging in to see what I was up to or went through a divorce or grieved when my baby died. God was always there. He had walked with me with every step. As in the beautiful poem *Footprints in the Sand*, God had carried me when I hadn't had the strength to put one foot in front of the other.

Not only that, but even though I let go of only one thing—my unhappiness—God exchanged it for three happy things: a sense of calm, a new freedom, and deliverance from the entrapment of unhappiness. That's the way he works—always giving us so much more than we give up.

I've often wondered why bad things happen even when we're trying to be good. But life's events have everything to do with God's mission to groom us and make us better and lead us into the full life he has for us. As he does this work, we are refined in the ovens of purification and polished.

God shattered the bonds of my unhappiness and set me on a course toward a centered life, and he can do the same for you. He comes to us so that we may have life and have it more abundantly (see John 10:10). Our richness of character, contentment with who we are, and yearning to achieve our personal best are aspirations that he has inscribed in our hearts. That's something we can hang our faith on!

Conclusion

Are you ready to take a journey through Erikson's life stages? This journey can help lead you to fulfill all the promises God has in store for you. As you exercise faith in him, he promises to give you a bright and promising future. His promises aren't always evident in our lives in the morning when we awake, but when we don't see any signs of God's promises being fulfilled, we need to rely upon our faith and rest in the fact that he is willing to work on our behalf—and that's a promise we can grab on to. Expect your journey to unfold truths and restoration one step at a time. Eventually your prayers will be answered.

I didn't get a horse when I prayed for it, but I did get a horse twelve years later when we lived on two acres in the country and not on a patch of common area in a congested city. God's timing is always perfect. He is faithful.

Action Point

The action point for this chapter is to follow the "exercise of a lifetime." This seven-step exercise through Erikson's life stages was a turning point in my life, and what it has done for me, it has the potential to do for you as well.

4

Igniting the Spark Inside You

Motivation is a fire from within. If someone else tries to light that fire under you, chances are it will burn very briefly.

STEPHEN R. COVEY

You have an appointment with your boss for your annual performance review. The first question that comes to your mind as you prepare for work that morning is, "What should I wear?" You rummage through your closet to find a special outfit or tie that will make you look like a standout. When you're dressed to kill, you stand for a few moments in front of the mirror, taking an assessment of yourself and making sure everything is in place. You approve of what you see and rush out the door feeling confident about your upcoming meeting.

This is an example of motivational behavior at work. We all perform these kinds of unintentional behaviors to meet many of our needs. When our needs are satisfied, we call it a good day. But there is an even greater kind of motivation that produces a joy unspeakable, and that happens when we *intentionally* identify motivational behaviors within us that will ignite a spark inside us that will kindle our passion, fulfill our dreams, and ultimately lead us to reach out and help others.

Experts say that we have a purpose—consciously or subconsciously—for what we do and what we say. But often we go about with our lives on autopilot and are not aware of the purpose behind our actions. If we're not aware of why we do what we do, how can we hold ourselves accountable for our actions?

The fact is, we're all motivated. The question is, what are we motivated toward? Motivation is the trigger that causes us to choose certain paths, behave certain ways, and cling to certain attitudes. If we want to live joyful lives, we need to figure out what motivates us to act as we do so that we can get rid of our incentive toward bad habits and instead become motivated toward our passion and purpose.

What Triggers Motivation?

My favorite snack growing up was Ritz crackers smothered with strawberry jam. The salty cracker piled high with red glistening jam was, in a word, delish! This was my mainstay until I became a teenager and lost my taste for the gooey treat. Whether I became too cool to eat childish concoctions or realized that they would be "a minute on the lips, forever on the hips," my desires changed—because my motives changed.

Have you ever wondered about *why* you are motivated to do the things you do in life?

At the core of all our motivation is need. When we can define our need, we can be motivated to break a bad habit or change a bad attitude.

But someone may ask, "What's the best way to pinpoint my need? Sometimes I feel driven by a lot of different needs."

The best way to identify a need is to give it a name. Dr. Phil, renowned TV talk-show host and psychiatrist, coined this term regarding dealing with bad habits: "Name it, then tame it." Giving attitude a name helps us understand our motivation. This understanding will guide us in analyzing the whys in what we do. Naming our need is the first step in changing our attitude and behavior.

But sometimes it can be challenging to deal with a need in one attempt. Some needs are hidden under layers of issues that we must work through to get to the bottom of a problem.

For example, it's a hot and humid summer day and you need to cool down. Nothing would relieve your discomfort better than a cold glass of lemonade. You pour the liquid over a stack of ice cubes in a tall glass. You drink it all in one long, smooth series of satisfying gulps. It hits the spot! But a few minutes later you're still hot. What happened? You identified part of the problem—but another part of the problem is still unresolved. Instead of another cold drink, you decide to sit in an air-conditioned room. Ah! Now you've solved your discomfort problem. Do you see how you addressed your need in layers: first the cold drink, then the cool room?

The key to understanding our motivation is to identify the layers of our need one at a time until our entire problem has been resolved. As each layer is exposed, we must be brave and resolve it. When we do, we can be prepared for something amazing to happen: the detoxification of our emotions.

When this takes place, we become able to see the next layer, and its solution is much easier than if our toxic emotions were controlling us. That's why it's important to remain patient through the process.

Life is a journey in which we're able to address our needs and monitor our motivation. When we take the necessary steps to travel along our life path, we will discover that at the end of our journey, we are better off than when we took our first step.

Motivation and Reward

If we are going to change a bad habit or a sour attitude, we must be motivated to do so. We want to change, but deep inside motivation is the desire for a reward. In other words, if we are truly going to change, we need to work toward a reward. The truth about reward, however, is that the one being motivated must consider the reward valuable enough to make a change. For the late-night snacker, avoiding a heart attack that could be caused by weight gain can be enough of a reward to break an eating habit.

But some rewards do not help us. They keep us stuck, preventing us from moving forward. A woman stays in an abusive relationship, for example. As miserable as she is, she stays in exchange for a reward, whether that be financial support, comfort with the known, or avoidance of ridicule. These abnormal rewards have created a comfort zone in which it's easier to stay than change.

When it comes to identifying rewards that will prompt us to change, be sure to challenge yourself to define and pursue only those rewards that motivate you toward your best life.

Zeroing In on What Motivates You So You Can Help Others

A modern analysis of human need has been developed by Tony Robbins, self-help author and motivational speaker. Robbins's concept of motivation leads one first to pursue one's own growth so that one can then serve others in a selfless, connected way. In other words, as we better understand our own needs, determine why we do what we do, and fix ourselves, we're then able to lend a hand to others. This reminds me of preflight instructions: put on your oxygen mask before helping someone else.

Whatever we do, no matter where or when, some need, some primal instinct, drives us. Robbins has identified six areas of human need:

- *Certainty*: being secure
- *Variety*: getting unstuck from routine with creativity and excitement
- *Self-esteem*/significance: feeling important, needed, wanted, and esteemed
- *Relationship*: loving and connecting with others
- *Growth*: becoming better, improving ourselves, stretching and excelling
- *Contribution*: moving beyond our pain and needs and focusing on the needs of others[1]

(For a more comprehensive definition of Robbins's needs list, please refer to appendix 2. While there, you may want to take a moment to find your own need in one or more areas. If you're at a tough place right now, this exercise can help define why you're doing what you're doing and why you're feeling a certain way.)

Several years ago I had an experience that required I fix myself before I could lend a hand to another. After a thirty-year career with a large corporation, I was burned out from the daily grind of a twelve-hour-a-day work schedule. I decided to retire, thinking that I wanted to do something totally different. I jotted down all the activities I never had time for: gardening, long walks on the beach, meeting friends for lunch, reading, cleaning the house. *Housecleaning?* What? Who in her right mind would want this activity as a must-have in a new chapter of life? I didn't have a good answer, but I kept housecleaning on the list—at the very end!

I believed my list could help me create the next chapter in my life—one without pressure, one in which my time was my own. But after I quit my job, I found it difficult to wean myself from the demands of a high-pressured career. Without my job I had lost my identity. I didn't know who I was, who I should be, who I wanted to be. I no longer recognized my life. I felt displaced.

I studied my new wish list, over and over again, hoping to find new meaning, new purpose, new direction. But it all seemed like busywork. Nothing appeared important. I wasn't solving problems, meeting deadlines, making budgetary decisions, influencing others, leading people. As I looked over the list, it seemed that what I had thought I wanted wasn't at all what I needed.

Goodness! What in the world was my fix?

I had learned from reading many self-help books that I must identify my motivation and get to the root issues of my attitudes and behavior. When I came across Robbins's theory, I decided to analyze my motivation and define who I was after making a big change in my life.

Looking at Robbins's concept of human needs, I believed that my current need was for self-esteem and significance—feeling important, needed, wanted, and esteemed. But in order to satisfy this need, I felt that I would have to return to work. That was the last place I wanted to be. What should I do? Reinvent myself?

I determined to name and tame my need. I rechecked my list for the umpteenth time (persistence pays off), but this time I asked, "What is the common denominator of all the activities on this list?" That's when I made an important discovery: my list was not busywork after all. It was productive. Planting and caring for a beautiful flower garden; long walks along the beach to connect with nature; reading a story that could whisk me away to another world; meeting friends for lunch with the luxury of time and not having to gulp down food and squeeze in conversation during a one-hour lunch break—imagine my surprise in discovering that this list expressed my greatest need: to breathe freely.

You're probably wondering about the housecleaning, right? I started to line through that, completely obliterating it from the list, but then I realized that even housecleaning was no longer the miserable chore it had previously been. I no longer had to rush through the arduous task. Rather, I could take my time and have the luxury of enjoying a few breaks here and there as I dealt with dirty dishes and dusty shelves.

Being freed from the pressure of time enabled me to understand the new motivation in my new life—to breathe freely—more clearly. I discovered that my need after quitting my job wasn't for self-esteem (feeling important, needed, wanted, and esteemed), as I had thought. It was for variety—getting unstuck from routine with creativity and excitement.

Naming my need after thirty years in corporate America and coming up with a new routine allowed my body, mind, and soul to relax. Once I was able to relax, I was able to detox from my insecurities about my new life and make the change from living in the fast lane to living a slower, more enriched lifestyle. In this renewed state of awareness, I was motivated to embark upon the new chapter in my life with clarity and purpose.

Sometimes we embark upon uncharted territory without giving it much thought. At other times fear and doubt cause us to withdraw from the very change we long for. The key in bringing about positive change in our lives is to be patient and persistent! I persistently pursued the source of my confusion and frustration after ending my thirty-year career, and this process led to the root need of my retired life. This is when I found stability in my life. Once I became balanced, joyous living automatically followed.

As we enter and leave different phases of our lives, however, it's important to understand that our needs will change. After leaving my career I needed variety for a season; once that need was fulfilled, another need blossomed and motivated me in a different direction—into another season. This new need was for contribution—the need to move beyond my own pain and needs and focus on the needs of others. I'm happy to report that this need led to the birth of my company, Cornerstone Management Skills—a motivational organization that allows me to travel nationally and internationally and encourage people to aspire to their highest levels of fulfillment and commitment to their intrapersonal growth—and it eventually led to the writing of this book. As I named my needs and took care of them, I then became able to help others.

Get Your Passion On

Oftentimes we hear people say they want more fire in their bellies. We all understand what that means: more passion; more fight; more emotional investment. It's about an extra inner drive, a burning to achieve success at any cost. When we have fire in our bellies, we become fed up with failure. We no longer find pleasure in excusing away our weaknesses. We are eager to try again or find a way to get better. We know we've got fire in our bellies when we get pushed down but don't stay there.

When our motivation is truly fired up, it is not a sometimes thing. It's an all-the-time thing. It's an attitude of being invincible. Unstoppable. It's not about being perfect or even powerful—it's simply about owning our own motivation. This kind of fire can't be blown out by a hefty wind.

When we take ownership of our own motivation, we become unstoppable. We stick to our guns, so to speak, knowing that our motivation belongs to us and us alone. We don't copy someone else's motivation, even if we think highly of it, because that person's need may be different from ours. It's like choosing not to get a hairstyle that we think fits perfectly on someone else's face, because it would look a bit off on ours. When we own our motivation, we're determined. And that makes us immovable.

People who are determinedly motivated see only the finish line. They are focused, persistent, and never distracted. They have found their sweet spots in their deepest needs. Nothing anyone says to discourage them will succeed. There is no stopping them.

This is how my business began. One day, as my need for breathing space began to be satisfied, I decided to take a serious look at a yearning that had been stirring in my heart for several months. After analyzing the pros and cons of entrepreneurship, I decided to start my company, Cornerstone Management Skills. My husband thought it was much ado about nothing. Only a façade. A mirror looking back at me without significance. "It would take too much work to market and manage a business," he said to me.

"You're supposed to be retired!" But I had fire in my belly, and nothing anyone said was going to deter me. I was unstoppable. Unshakable. Unmovable.

Cornerstone was my dream. My vision became my passion. But it wasn't my husband's, so it is easy to understand why he didn't see my finish line. But I learned an important concept while pursuing my dream. In order to see my dream to its finish line, I had to ignore the naysayers (as hard as that was toward my dear husband), and keep my eyes on the prize. As Cornerstone began to grow during the first three years, I was blessed with speaking engagements both nationally and internationally. My husband began to recognize the potential in Cornerstone and to see its purpose and vision. I'm happy to announce that he now plays an important role in enhancing existing programs in my business and creating new ones as well. He holds the prestigious title of chief guidance officer! He loves his role and now understands my passion.

Let passion ignite the powerful fire in your belly. This level of motivation doesn't see roadblocks. It only sees the prize. It equips us with the drive to reach for the sky and let our fingertips touch our personal star.

You may feel stuck right now; what you really want may seem a long distance away. But don't get discouraged with your journey. Stay strong—run your race. Never give up on your dream. Allow divine intervention to move you forward. In time doors will begin to open. God will see to it.

Conclusion

What motivates you? What drives your behavior? It's important to identify your needs so that you can deal with motivations that lead to bad habits and feed the passion that leads to your dreams.

When it comes to the matter of dreams, do you have a spark brewing deep inside you? Have you identified the driving need that will enable you to reach your dream? Are you hesitant? Fearful?

God knows the plans he has for you. The core of *his* motivation is to give you hope and a future (see Jeremiah 29:11). When you trust in him, nothing can keep you from fueling your motivation and accomplishing the task he has placed before you. He stands at the steering wheel of your dreams; he is the source of your motivation. Let him take the lead as you press in to your passion.

Action Points

Why does motivation play an integral part in your behavior and attitudes?

Identify a need you have, and determine how it motivates you. Is the motivation highlighting a behavior you'd like to change? If so, how would you go about doing that?

Robbins's theory of motivation helped me tremendously to bridge my time from career to the next season in my life. If you're in a similar transition and need direction, need to identify your motivation, I encourage you to discover your need in Robbins's list. Chart your journey to a new purpose and passion.

5

Accountability Fuels Your Goals

When we have begun to take charge of our lives, to own ourselves, there is no longer any need to ask permission of someone.

GEORGE O'NEIL

Like most adults, I was taught accountability early in life. Every time I knelt inside the confessional booth at church, my little heart nearly burst with conviction, as if a crooked finger were scolding me, "You could be outside playing instead of kneeling in this scary, dark booth." My chubby hands clutched together, I'd scan the darkness, wide eyed, wondering, "Where's the light switch anyway?"

What sounded like the eerie creak of a coffin lid rising echoed through the room as the priest slid open the wooden window panel. My breath froze in my chest as I tried to decipher his silhouette, wondering if he was the nice priest or the mean one. After confessing all, I braced myself as the priest vomited a long list of items for penance. His restitution gymnastics ranged from saying the rosary three times at the altar while kneeling on a wooden step (the hard step was a real knee killer) to walking the Stations of the Cross twice. (After hearing all that, I decided that I must have gotten the mean priest.) My nine-year-old conscience regretted the day I was born.

Once the painful experience was forgotten, however—it generally took three days at least—I was back to my deplorable, unaccountable self.

Simply stated, accountability is being responsible for our behavior. Our quick-satisfaction society has little room for accountability. Be prepared for a blank stare when teenagers are asked if they're accountable to anyone. It's sometimes difficult for adults as well to be accountable for their behavior, decisions, and attitudes. We should always behave responsibly, right? We're taught this from a young age. But accountability is one of the toughest life principles to master.

Perhaps the poster child in capriciousness is Mike Tyson, the heavyweight champion of the world, who was the youngest boxer to win the WBC, WBA, and IBF heavyweight titles. He was twenty years old. Fortune and fame, however, eventually puffed him up enough that he angrily bit off a competitor's ear. He admits that he had no boundaries. After a life-transforming experience with the death of his four-year-old daughter, Mike was brought to his knees, and for the first time in his undisciplined life, he realized that the greatest heavyweight champion could not hold up under the tragedy of loss and regret.

Today it can be said that Mike Tyson, the undisputed heavyweight champion of the world, has now become the poster child for accountability. He considers himself undeniably rich in peace and integrity, living happily with his wife and two young children. He credits his family for keeping him accountable. Who would have thought in the acme of his uncontrollable behavior that one day he would be a man of honor? Think about it! If Mike can do it, anyone can.

Where do we start with this ambition to become accountable? This quality, otherwise known as personal responsibility, is vital in our journey toward a balanced life. The first step in cultivating this characteristic is self-discipline.

Self-Discipline

The idea of self-discipline creates a word picture for me. I see a path—some parts of it are straight and wide; others are curvy, hilly, gnarly. The perimeter of the pathway is lined with safety cones. The idea is to stay on the road, not to get sidetracked. This isn't always easy, but we have an advocate that can help us keep focused: self-discipline. It is the inner voice that beckons, "Stay focused! Heed the cones! Don't miss the warning signs!" Accountability is largely fueled by self-discipline, and it can help us overcome any nasty habit. It wipes out procrastination and lukewarm commitment.

Self-discipline is one of the most important and useful skills we can have. This skill is essential in every area of life, because it gives us the power to stick to our decisions.

What words come to mind when you think of self-discipline? Experts say the most common words are "perseverance," "self-control," "persistence," "willpower"; they also describe it as resisting distractions or temptations, or trying over and again until we accomplish our goals. All these descriptors point to a person who is driven, unshakable, a taskmaster. Being driven doesn't mean being harsh toward ourselves or living limited, restrictive lifestyles; self-discipline means self-control, which is a sign of inner strength.

Unfortunately, self-discipline isn't developed overnight.

Building Self-Discipline

As with anything worthwhile, self-discipline takes work, sometimes hard work. We might think of self-discipline as a muscle. Use it or lose it, as the saying goes. The more we exercise our sense of determination, the stronger it becomes. Soon it will be strong enough that little effort will need to be exerted. But as in any physical regime, muscles need to be consistently exercised.

We can think about building our self-discipline muscle as we would strengthen our physical muscles. All kinds of exercises can strengthen every muscle in our bodies, but one of the most effective ways to build physical muscle is through weight training. We shouldn't start by lifting a hundred pounds, nor should we expect immediate and powerful strength. Success in weight training is to progressively build muscle. This means lifting weights that are close to our limit, then increasing them as we get stronger. If we keep working out with the same weights, we won't get any stronger. Similarly, if we don't challenge ourselves, we won't gain higher levels of discipline.

The first step toward self-discipline is understanding its importance to our lives. Take a moment to jot down a list of areas in your life in which you're undisciplined. When I made my own list, I found that one of my most undisciplined behaviors involved my mouth. I have a bad habit of being sarcastic with little regard for others' feelings. One day while reading my Bible, I came across a verse about being accountable for every word I spoke. *Every word? I'm in deep trouble!* I thought. The verse went on to say that each of us would have to give an *account* of what we said. At that moment I decided to clean up my conversation and to speak from my heart and not my head. This self-discipline paid off, because it changed my critical attitude toward others. Then I began wondering about other areas in my life that were undisciplined. One by one, as I searched my behavior under the flashlight of accountability, other bad behaviors popped up. Through this process I discovered that growing in self-discipline was critical to leading a happy life.

The second step toward self-discipline is getting started. Sometimes that alone takes discipline. If you've been procrastinating, please stop. If you don't start, just think what you'll miss: opportunities to plot your course to a balanced life, live joyously, increase self-esteem, and stand at the top of your world! Wow!

The third step is being kind to ourselves. Don't push too hard as you build self-discipline. Remember, self-discipline is gained by progression, level by level. Some days you will do really well, while other days you will need extra effort. Be kind by forgiving yourself on days when your devotion declines. And don't forget to love yourself unconditionally. Loving yourself will cover a myriad of oversights and wrong decisions.

Love will increase patience, and when we're patient, we'll be willing to give ourselves a second chance. Endurance and tolerance are further definitions for patience. These terms remind me of an athlete preparing for a race. He or she works out for hours each day and runs countless times around a field track. Endurance and tolerance create victory. Without patience the athlete wouldn't have enough self-discipline to accomplish his or her goal. Patience gives the athlete the inspiration that leads to success.

The fourth step toward self-discipline is not comparing ourselves with other people. No one is exactly like anyone else, and making unfair comparisons will only cause discouragement. For example, if you think you are weak, everyone else will seem stronger than you are. There's no point in doing this to yourself! It's a futile exercise. Discipline yourself to look at where you are now, and aim to get better.

The fifth step is taking periodic assessments of our self-discipline plan. Let's say you want to develop an exercise program. You plan the place, time, duration, and an exercise regime. You decide to work out at five thirty in the morning for sixty minutes. The first day is a breeze. Then the second day comes. You can barely get out of bed. Your muscles are screaming! The last thing you want to do is to work those muscles again. So you decide to stay in bed—and you feel as though you've failed. Now you're discouraged. But you need to keep in mind that you exercised the first day. Perhaps two consecutive days are too much.

Sometimes it's easy for us to overestimate our capability when we chart out a plan. We have a tendency to set our goals too high. I call this "my eyes were bigger than my plan." Instead of giving up, we need to rethink our plan. We should not scold ourselves; instead, we should reassess the situation and then decide what's best for our success. By raising the bar just a little at a time, we can stay within our capabilities and grow stronger over time. Just as weight training is a methodical, progressive work toward its goals, so too is developing and maintaining self-discipline.

The Enemies of Self-Discipline and How to Squash Them

The enemies of self-discipline come in different shapes and sizes, but their common thread is mental poison. When you have decided to make behavioral or attitudinal changes in your life, has something come up to hamper your efforts or enthusiasm? Check the list of enemies below, and see if you've opened the door to any of the following mental poisons:

- *Laziness*: a state of sluggishness or the lack of energy to start or to stay on a plan
- *Procrastination*: to put off, delay—the "tomorrow" attitude
- *Excuses*: finding a reason why something *cannot* work and letting this keep you from trying (Remember, the harsh truth about excuses is that only losers make them. Losers never aspire to improve their lives; they are entrapped within the walls of their conjured-up false justifications.)
- *Negativity*: focusing on negative thoughts rather than on positive ones, creating a self-fulfilling prophecy
- *Cynicism*: questioning the value, appropriateness, timing, or effectiveness of any potential goal or solution
- *Escapism*: diverting your attention to other activities, typically those that bring more short-term pleasure

Now that we're aware of the different types of enemies we can experience, let's take a stand and find ways to squash the enemy and use it to strengthen our self-discipline muscle! A simple and effective technique to strengthening our willpower is to do things that we would rather avoid doing, whether due to laziness, procrastination, lack of inner strength and assertiveness, shyness, or other similar reasons. By carrying out such actions, we become stronger in spite of our inner resistance and reluctance.

Are you ready to roll up your sleeves and tackle these enemies? Read through the following list of exercises that will help to straighten your self-discipline posture.

Give up your seat. You are sitting in a bus or train, and an old man or woman or a pregnant lady walks in. Stand up and give up your seat, even if you prefer to stay seated. Do it not just because it is polite but because it is something you are reluctant to do. This is an exercise in overcoming the resistance of your body, mind, and feelings.

Take control of the kitchen. The dishes in the sink need washing, and you postpone the job for later. Get up and wash them now. Don't let laziness control you. When you know that in this way you are actually strengthening yourself, it becomes easier to take immediate action, despite laziness and the desire to procrastinate.

Climb the stairway to success. If you have the choice of going up the elevator or climbing the stairs, choose the stairs. Do this, however, only if the story you are going to isn't too high and you are in good physical condition.

Personal Accountability Techniques

The secret to the successful and happy life we are climbing toward is to be consistent in working on our goals. But try as we might to work on our goals, we all have many tugs and pulls in our lives that make it a challenge to stay focused. I've developed several accountability techniques that have helped me get to the finish line of my goals. If you'd like more information on ways to cultivate personal accountability, please turn to appendix 3, where you'll find more details on the following topics:

- *Creating personal accountability goal cards.* This is a convenient tracking system to monitor your goals.
- *Reviewing your goals.* Our lives tend to become incredibly busy and it's helpful to review your goals and keep them fresh in your mind.
- *Growing your character to reach your goals.* Wonder why you meet some goals and not others? This section will give you a few ideas.
- *Building an accountability partnership.* Add more fun and success to your journey by inviting someone to keep you on track.
- *Writing affirmation statements and tag-along sentences.* An affirmation is a thought that will help spur you to accomplish your goal; a tag-along statement is a sentence that you create to reinforce the affirmation statement.
- *Giving yourself special recognition.* Plan a special acknowledgment for yourself when you meet certain milestones in your journey.
- *Creating a memory bank.* Jot down your successes. These events will encourage you to stay persistent.

Have Fun!

With all the diligent work it takes to stay on task with our goals, we sometimes lose sight of *being* in the busyness of *doing*. One way to energize our effort to succeed is to find ways to have fun!

One of the values of my company, Cornerstone Management Skills, is to have fun. This concept is important to my success, longevity, and sometimes my sanity. Having fun, regardless of the doldrums or challenges of a task, helps me take the bite out of the seriousness I may have imposed on a situation.

Fun helps me approach both my work life and personal life in a more relaxed and enjoyable way. When I'm relaxed, I think better. When I think better, I'm more creative. It's hard to have fun and think negatively at the same time. It's like trying to look both up and down at the same time. Impossible! Fun can relieve stress, help us maintain balance, and enable us to avoid burnout.

Why do children know how to have fun? Because they are masters at play. As adults, we tend to lose the playful part of our lives. It's not automatic for us. Maybe we shouldn't take ourselves so seriously. Loosen up. Laugh more. If you have a dog, play with it; throw a toy around or play chase. Listen to music. Watch a comedy. Take a quiet walk. Can you think of more ways to have fun?

Conclusion

When I think of self-discipline and accountability, I think of a marriage. These two character traits form an inseparable union. We can't have one without the other, as the old song "Love and Marriage" made popular by Frank Sinatra in 1955 nostalgically tells us.

Try to think about self-discipline without accountability and accountability without self-discipline. It's like trying to bake a cake without turning on the oven. Don't forget that building accountability is a process—it takes time to grow our self-discipline muscles. Experts say that a disciplined person is a happy person. Think about yourself after you've been disciplined, whether by yourself or someone else. Did the discipline pay off? Did it make you happy? Did willpower motivate you to hard work because the payoff was worth all the effort?

Are you ready to get happy? Don't waste another day. Welcome accountability into your life.

Action Points

To respond to this chapter's action points, it would be helpful to first read through the personal accountability techniques outlined in appendix 3.

How would you define accountability?

Could an area in your life use some self-discipline? Describe it in one sentence.

Now that you've identified an area that needs self-discipline, what can you do to build a self-discipline goal?

Why is it important to maintain personal accountability around your goals? Consider accountability techniques: achieve, review, match character to goals, etc.

Name one person who could be an accountability partner for you. What do you like best about this person?

In your journey toward a joyful, balanced life, it's important to form specific goals. Create an affirmation statement for one of your life goals.

Now that you have an affirmation statement, create a tag-along statement.

6

Changing from the Inside Out

The art of living lies not in eliminating but in growing with troubles.

BERNARD BARUCH

We don't always like what we see when we look in the mirror. We think a little tuck here or there might improve our appearance. Some people resort to magic creams and makeup products to enhance their features. Others lean toward cosmetic surgery. All these efforts are temporary by virtue of the pull of gravity and the aging process that eventually forces every area of our bodies to sag.

What really matters when we want change in our lives is what's happening inside us. It's worth our time to work more on the internal than the external. Our bodies serve as houses for our souls, which live forever—long after our bodies expire. Doesn't it seem worthwhile in our efforts to achieve balanced, happy lives to work on those things that are lasting rather than looking for quick and easy fixes?

When I was in my early twenties, I was hooked on self-help books. The first one I read was *Fragrance of Beauty* by Joyce Landorf Heatherley. She wrote of her identical twin aunts who had extremely different personalities. One was vivacious, fun loving, always laughing. The other was serious, angry, deeply unhappy. As her aunts became elderly, Joyce witnessed a dramatic difference in how they looked. Deepened lines covered virtually every inch of the angry aunt's face; her eyes had a mean glare; her mouth scrunched into a tight circle; her hair appeared dry and coarse. The happy twin, however, had a vibrancy about her. Her eyes gleamed, and the loveliness of her soul arose as a fragrance of beauty.

Sure, we can get a new hairstyle, wear a new outfit, or use a new line of super anti-aging cosmetics, but these are all efforts to change our outsides. Although changing our "package" can be important, changing from the inside out is critical for living a satisfying life.

Change Takes Determination

One of the challenges in every life is that while we desire to grow in character and aspire to healthy attitudes, doing so is not always easy. Personal growth requires that we be brave enough to ask, "What can I learn and how can I grow through difficulties and hard times?" Too often we resist answering these tough questions in our passion to live safely. Shining the spotlight on and inspecting the gems we could cultivate from the hardships we have endured will take us one step in the direction of changing from the inside out.

Our quest to change from the inside out is better served when we see ourselves as God desires to see us: as victorious, more than conquerors. The reality, however, is that most of us focus on our weaknesses and not our strengths. Our perception of who we are and whether we're capable of working hard to change our character will determine how well we travel into uncharted territory in our lives.

Many times I have stood in front of a mirror and looked deep into my eyes, and I've tried to critically and honestly examine my strengths and weaknesses. Whenever I've done this, I've found that God has created me with things I like about myself and things I don't. What I need to realize, though, is that the culmination of my total person has been created well. When I recognize this, I jumpstart my effort to change.

What do you see when you look in a mirror? Do you see someone God created well or someone God created as junk? Your answer is critical to how you see yourself—and how you see yourself is how you'll react during tough times.

One day I called my eighty-four-year-old grandmother. For several years she had been confined to her bed or a wheelchair; she could no longer feed or care for herself. I asked her how she was doing. She thought for a moment and replied, "Every day I learn something new." *What? Every day?* I thought. *What can she learn from her bed?*

But over the years I thought about what she had told me that day—"Every day I learn something new." Her mind was sharp. She was progressive in her thinking. She never entertained negative thoughts. Her faith was strong. She must have looked for ways to better herself even at her age and in her limited condition. In order for her to consistently look for something new every day, she must have had an open mind—she was hungry for newness of life. She knew that as long as she was alive (she passed away at age ninety-two), she had work to do.

That's true for all of us—as long as we're alive, we have work to do. As long as we're breathing, we have opportunities to hone our skills. Our lives always contain unfinished business. We are on a continual journey to reengineer ourselves—to be renewed, redesigned, and transformed from the inside out.

The Impossible Finish Line

Depending on the depth of change we want to effect in our climb toward balance, the finish line can seem light years away. Sometimes our goals seem enormous—the size of an elephant. But hold on! Don't be discouraged! There's a simple plan.

We can break up that elephant into smaller, more manageable tasks. No challenge is completely overwhelming if it is broken down properly. We need to identify the key pieces of the growth we want to see in our lives and then tackle them individually.

Regardless of the problems we want to overcome, the first thing we need to do is reduce them to their simplest forms so that we can know exactly what we're dealing with. While we're doing this, we can ask ourselves questions to make sure we're focusing on the right things. Once we have simplified and right-sized a problem, we can put together a plan to actually solve it.

Our plans may include due dates—the dates we want to accomplish our goals by. From that date, we can back up to where we are today—at the starting line—and assign a pocket of time each day to work on the matter until we reach the due date. We shouldn't forget to pad our schedules for any surprises that may come up. One of the greatest obstacles to reaching the finish line is not allowing ourselves enough time to accomplish our goals. The added stress will make us discouraged and make it easier for us to give up altogether.

Getting to Work—and Staying with It

Once the elephant is cut up into manageable pieces, it's time to roll up our sleeves and get to work on our goals for change. In the beginning we are generally motivated and excited, but during the journey we can hit the wall and lose our oomph. What should we do when this happens?

First, we need to focus exclusively on the piece we're working on. Don't worry about the rest of the elephant. Work patiently, methodically—go from piece to piece—and soon the entire monstrous task will be done.

Second, we need to maintain the same determination and gusto we had when we first decided to make a change. One way we can do this is to be selective over the thoughts we think and the words we say. Words are powerful, and this is what the well-known adage "garbage in, garbage out" means: our thoughts, whether positive or negative, will eventually show up in our behavior. We're not only the subject of change—the ones being changed for the better. We're also the recipient of it—we become our own benefactors of the improvements we've made to ourselves.

Third, we need to seize all our fortitude and patience to nurture and encourage ourselves to stay on task.

Finally, divine rescue is ready at our call to make a way when we may lose our focus.

Get in the Groove

Developing consistent good behavior is one of the most powerful advocates for helping us stay on the path of change. When we can trust ourselves to regularly exhibit good behavior, we can rely on creating a routine that promotes our character strengths and minimizes our weaknesses. Once we establish a behavior routine, it tells our brain, "This is what needs to happen." Our brain will get in the groove and work with us instead of against us.

Our brain works best when we feed it consistent behavior. This is why it is helpful to focus on one reliable ritual in our quest to attain our goals. For example, if your goal is to exercise, create a plan to wake up every day at a certain time. Or if you want a cigarette, take a drink of water every time instead. The biggest ally when it comes to accomplishing change is replacing our bad behaviors with good ones.

This will encourage us by providing a new determination to guide us. We'll be ready to work out at five thirty in the morning instead of trying to steal a few more winks. We'll choose a drink of water instead of smoking up our insides. Each time we do the replacement deed, we tell our brain that *this* is our new behavior, and because repetition helps reshape the brain, our brains will eventually get in the groove and work with us.

No Room for Perfectionists

When we're trying to motivate ourselves, it helps if we are grateful for the fact that we're actually thinking about making a change. As we move forward, we should not be hard on ourselves but allow ourselves to be "good enough." Perfectionism can undo what we're trying to achieve. For example, if we're tired one day, we may want to reduce our exercise plan by ten minutes, but we feel as though these few minutes will take a bite out of our resolve. Here's a question to ask our perfectionism: "Is ten minutes going to make that much difference?" A perfectionist may say, "Ten minutes are ten precious minutes. Every minute counts! Shame on you if you decide to cheat. Cheater! Cheater! Cheater!" But when we step out of our perfectionism, we become more sensible and reasonable with ourselves.

Here's the difference between perfectionism and sensibility: perfectionism will burn us out, spin our wheels; sensibility will encourage us to regroup and recognize the importance of being realistic in our effort to stay on task. Sensibility may say, "Think balance. If exercising ten minutes less is what your body needs today, then do it." If we feel stronger the next time we exercise, we can consider adding the ten minutes we missed on our weaker day.

Shout It Out!

We need to go out and tell somebody about the positive changes in our lives. In fact, we can go ahead and tell several people—a spouse, parents, okay, even our pets. We're more powerful when others understand our mission. They can become a huge asset to helping us maintain accountability.

Sometimes we feel lonely on the path to change. Some days are less than we hope they will be. It's easy to pull away from people. But that won't serve us well. Rather, we must be accountable for our progress and find an accountability partner or someone else we trust. They'll be happy to encourage, sustain, and keep us afloat.

Are You Listening?

The ability to take advice is important in our efforts to accomplish our goals and live joyously. *Giving* advice, conversely, is the responsibility of our accountability partners; we should let our accountability partners know that their responsibilities are to be our coach, help us stay on track, and support our goals. Once they do their part to guide us, however, it's time for us to do ours: listen!

We need to listen to their advice. When the effort to change becomes overwhelming, and sometimes it can, it's easy to get on the defensive and make excuses for ourselves. But the job description of our partners is not to hear excuses; it's to coach us. The exchange is simple: they coach; we listen.

No Pity Parties, Please!

Ever notice that a pity party is often a party of one? Why is that? First, let's consider the nature of a pity party: it's self-centered, self-accommodating, and self-indulgent. Really, who wants to attend a party like that? But unhappy and unwelcoming as it may be, we often tend to give in to our strained emotions and sulk in this party.

My eighty-year-old high-energy grandmother suffered from crippling rheumatoid arthritis that confined her to a wheelchair. Crooked fingers, weak hands, swollen feet and knees, and constant pain required her to exert extra effort to complete a simple task. But I never heard a word of complaint from her. One day when I asked her how she was doing, she said, "If God gave me this body, then he'll have to give me the strength to live today." I listened to her with dropped jaw. You'd have done the same if you could have seen her at her worst, rocking and groaning with the pain that racked her body. Even in such a chronic state of despair, she radiated a positive attitude. It kept her spirits high. She enjoyed inner peace because she refused to entertain self-pity.

To succeed at change, we must become a creating force in our own lives. If we don't, the dreadful habit of believing that we are victims can interfere with our success. Victims see themselves through foggy lenses. Their mind-sets are always negative. They are the injured parties, the casualties, the premier sufferers, and the severely wounded.

The only way for us to avoid pity parties is to understand our circumstances. We should ask, "Do I believe I am a victim? If so, how do I change my mind-set? How can I see past my pain?" If we were to search people and their predicaments, we'd probably find someone who is worse off than we are—someone who would give anything to be in our situations.

A Heart of Gratitude

Ever try to be happy and sad at the same time? Thankful and grumpy? Smiling and frowning? It's impossible. True thanksgiving sets us on a straight pathway where negativity can't exist.

Positive thoughts have the power to crush negativity. You may be thinking, *It's so hard to get rid of negative thoughts. They're like a snowball—they get bigger and bigger.* Ah, but there is a solution. We can reprogram our brains by thinking positive thoughts. Eventually the positive thoughts will dominate our minds, and the negative thoughts will be crushed.

When we crush negativity, it's surprising how our positive thoughts will lead to thankfulness. Can you see how simply changing an attitude can spiral upward to a happy life?

The act of thanksgiving has the power to lift our spirits and plant a smile in our hearts. It has the power to keep us positive and happy. By being grateful we take control over any struggles against change. A thankful heart tells our brain that there is hope—that we're going to make it.

Some years ago Oprah introduced the idea of keeping a gratitude journal as a way of tracking the good things that spurred a thankful heart. Her plan was simple: jot down five things to be thankful for every day. Everyone seemed to be on this journal craze. A friend gave me a journal for my birthday. Every morning, I'd jot down five "thankful things." This methodical exercise helped set my compass in the right direction for the entire day. Whenever something negative or unexpected bombed my day, I reacted defensively, but because of the thankful exercise I'd done that morning, I was able to stop the bad attitude and recall how many important things were going right in my life.

Sometimes, try as we might, we can find absolutely nothing to be thankful for. Sorrow clouds our vision. We look at life through the heavy fog of despair. We feel too small for the enormity of our problem. How can anyone find a speck of anything to be thankful for under dreadful circumstances? Here's a tip: go to the simple basics in life. Reach out and allow your soul to touch nature. Go outside and take a deep breath of fresh air, and let it settle deep within your being. Gaze at the beauty of the outdoors that God created for us to enjoy. But don't stop there—the expanse of nature beckons us to enjoy its breadth, length, and height.

Listen to the sweet serenade of birds singing, and let their song lift the heaviness from your heart. Look at the trees, and notice how their branches point heavenward. Lift your arms to the sky, and let a note of thanksgiving rise up from your soul. Close your eyes, take in another breath, and let it out slowly. Try to think of one more thing to be thankful for.

I recently had lunch with a friend who shared with me how exhausted she was from battling allergies. Before meeting me she had prayed for a change in her attitude. After praying, in her mind's ear she heard an old church hymn, "Whatever my lot, thou hast taught me to say, 'It is well, it is well with my soul.'"[1] She sang the chorus as she drove to the restaurant. At first it wasn't well with her soul. Nothing was well. But God had given her a song, so she sang it over again until wellness saturated her being deep within. By the time she pulled into the parking lot, her attitude was positive. And being positive, her aches and pains weren't as bothersome to her. We enjoyed a wonderful meal and conversation.

Dwell in Healthy Reality

Changing from the inside out is about finding a place of balance. This is also known as healthy reality. Balance means standing emotionally on two feet.

An experiment will help illustrate the healthy reality concept: Try standing on one foot for a few minutes. Soon you'll start to wobble. Just before tottering over, put your other foot down, and shift your weight evenly onto both feet. See how much stronger you are—balanced and centered.

The next time the winds of challenge try to throw you off, stand solid emotionally on both feet, and enjoy renewed strength, confidence, and vigor. You'll know when you're living in healthy reality when words like "fear," "anxiety," and "doubt" are no longer part of your normal vocabulary. You'll feel inner poise, because the core of your being will be in balance. Destructive winds of negativity cannot budge you in the slightest.

Living in healthy reality makes us strong from the tops of our heads all the way down to our big toes! It's that powerful!

Nurture Your Mind

The tender care given to a new garden is the same technique that works for growing our character from the inside out. Before seeds can be planted in a garden, the earth must be carefully cultivated, making the soil perfect for planting. Our minds also need to be cultivated, making them ready for core values to be sown. A gardener, once she has made the soil ready, will decide how to design her garden. Once we have made our minds ready, we will be ready to become the architect of change.

After the seeds have been planted and new life begins to appear, we have to tend to the growing qualities in our lives. How is a garden tended? Experts say by consistent watering, fertilizing, and squashing of bugs. This same kind of tender care can translate into caring for seeds of change in our minds: creating breathing space, maintaining good thoughts, and squashing bad attitudes. This special care applies to growing and nurturing ourselves from the inside out.

Let's say you need to get better control of your budget. You've set a goal to cut back on shopping sprees after work on Friday. You plan a new shopping budget and decide how many Fridays you'll shop and what you'll do on other Fridays to occupy yourself. Now you're set—you're energized; nothing can get in your way. But it does! And you have another failed attempt at turning over a new leaf. What went wrong—again?

A law of nature says that if adequate water and care are given to seeds, they'll grow; assumedly, if we do our part as gardeners, the seeds will do theirs. But sometimes a gardener stops watering, fertilizing, and squashing bugs—and when that happens, the plants will die. We can do the same thing when we hit a wall in the middle of achieving our goal: we stop nurturing the soil of our minds, and we end up going backward instead of forward, or we quit completely. It's a condition called self-sabotage.

Warnings of Self-Sabotage

Failure to bring about the change we have set about to achieve is generally not for lack of good intentions. There simply comes a time when the honeymoon with our new goal is over, and it becomes easy for us to drop the ball. Failure then causes us to feel bad, even guilty. As we beat ourselves up over our lack of willpower, laziness, or weakness, sabotage seems to win again and again.

Inner scolding, worry, and angst are always in the background of our brains, and when we're confronted with something new, unfamiliar, or threatening, these voices rev up. Our brain tells us to give up—we're making life too hard. But there's a deeper issue: our brain does not like change. The brain becomes uncomfortable with change because change causes a state of imbalance. The brain wants to get back to where it was before the change, even if it means keeping a bad habit.

So how do we ward off the negative forces within us that want to sabotage our growth so that we can still work toward change? Let's do a little soul searching.

To understand how our brains function during change, it helps to create what I call a "mental map." To do this four-step process, we must first identify a life goal. Then, second, we can consider all the ways we may routinely sabotage ourselves—in other words, all the ways we tend to put a wrench in our efforts. Third, once our sabotage behavior is revealed, we can pinpoint what is causing us to stop nurturing our goals, which will help us as we seek to put a stop to its menacing destruction.

After we've plotted the first three points on our mental maps and determined ways in which we have been sabotaging ourselves, it's time to work on the fourth and final step: dealing with the anxiety that feeds our self-sabotage. Anxiety is a natural feeling, because we face unknowns as we try to reach our goals. Sure, we expect change, improvement, but what does that really mean? Success? Failure?

One of the most common responses to attempted change is fear. It is the root problem of anxiety. Fear can paralyze our ambition and destroy our quests to reach goals. But once fear is resolved, anxiety goes away. Whenever self-sabotage creeps into my thoughts, I ask, "In this situation, what do I know for sure?" In that very moment, in the midst of my calamity and anxiety, I find a nugget of truth about myself, and that truth is embedded in "what I know for sure." Analyzing this question anchors assurance and sets us on solid ground. Please do not allow fear to stand in your way. Embrace the strength that God has already planted inside you. Allow faith to carry you forward. Never, ever give up on yourself.

Angie's world dissolved into a nightmare when her forty-year-old son died of an acute heart attack. She was on vacation when he died. She felt guilty that she had been having fun as he died in the hospital among strangers. Had she been home, she could have helped him, and perhaps he would still be alive. Her thoughts were consumed with what she should have done, what she could have done.

When you have been faced with a traumatic situation, has your mind raced in different directions? This phenomenon often occurs when we are under great duress, and our thoughts become uncontrollable as the brain jumps from thought to thought at lightning speed. Our thoughts frantically look for something to hold on to, but their erratic speed causes us to think in fragments. When our brains attempt to make sense of the chaos, they hang on to an enormous pile of what ifs.

In order to help ground Angie's impulsive thoughts, I asked her, "Right now, in this very moment, what do you know for sure about Charlie?"

Angie was quiet for a long time, tears streaming down her face. Then she slowly answered, "I know for sure that Charlie was on a good path. He had finally realized that he wanted better. He had found a job he loved. He had become active as a high-school leader at his church. He had reconciled with his teenage daughter. One time they even watched *Next Top Model* together. He hated that show," she recalled, smiling, "but it was the time with his daughter that mattered."

I encouraged her to hold on to what she knew for sure. It would help her remember the last good days of Charlie's life. Whenever the dark days inched back into her thoughts, as they inevitably would, she could recall those things she knew for sure and let them become her strength. This was an important exercise for her, because the good days that Charlie had experienced had given him strength, and that sense of strength could be Angie's as well.

You may be at a tough place today in which anxiety or some other obstacle is sabotaging your thoughts. Give yourself a break. Fill your mind with those things you know for sure. You'll begin to realize a ray of hope in a hopeless situation. After all, that's what you really need, isn't it? That small ray of hope.

Become More Patient

Although patience was discussed in chapter 1, it warrants another mention here. Patience is like the gasoline in a car: it enables us to go where we need to go. In order to drive to a destination, our gas tank must be filled enough to take us to our targeted location. To go the distance in our journey of change from the inside out, we must have a healthy supply of patience.

But what does having patience really mean? Sometimes when we're steeped forehead high in impatience, getting a grip on patience can be nearly impossible. What's the fix? Well, let's look for another word for patience. Sometimes changing our vocabulary can bring a fresh thought to our efforts. Other terms for "patience" might be, for example, "tolerance," "endurance," "staying power," "persistence," "fortitude," "serenity," "no complaints." Find a word that you can hang on to—a word that fits you best and that you can pack in your suitcase as you travel toward a balanced life.

Remember, the journey to improve our lives is never a quick fix. It's not fast travel. Working toward our goals becomes a smoother ride when we are patient with ourselves. The more patient we are, the more accepting we will be, especially if we fall off the wagon. Without patience, a goal seeker's life is extremely frustrating. Little things begin to annoy and irritate. Patience adds a dimension of ease and acceptance and tends to mellow out our struggles. Patience says, "You messed up. Forgive yourself. Dust yourself off. Move onward."

Conclusion

When you determine to change bad habits or attitudes, you change your character, which resides deep inside your soul. When you change your character, you change from the inside out. The beauty that blossoms from within your being will radiate to your outside. Allow divine truths from strong attributes in your personal-quality DNA—integrity, love, patience, kindness, gratitude—to change you from the inside out.

Action Points

Complete the following sentence: "It's important to change from the inside out because _____ ."

Why is being a perfectionist like a poison to your efforts to self-improvement?

Think of a goal that will help you change from the inside out, and list three things that you can be thankful for once you accomplish your goal:

My goal:

I will be thankful for:
1.
2.
3.

Have you had a chance to create a mental map? If not, perhaps now is a good time. Please refer to appendix 4.

7

Breaking the Beast Hidden Deep in a Habit

Man becomes a slave to his constantly repeated acts. What he at first chooses, at last compels.

ORISON SWETT MARDEN

We don't awake excited each day saying, "I'm going to schedule coffee today with my habit," or, "My calendar has more time for my habit this afternoon." Rather, we go about our lives, not giving any thought to our habits, when suddenly out of the blue something stirs within us, and—bam!—we're up to our ears in a habit that over time has come to dominate our lives.

"The devil made me do it!" This saying was coined in the 1970s by then popular comedian Flip Wilson as a reason for bad behavior. Blaming the devil for missteps brought loads of laughter, but behind the message is this naked truth: it's our own attitude that creates our behavior. The devil is blamed for a lot of things, but the way we behave is on us.

Sometimes our habits keep us in bondage, causing us to do things we don't want to do or preventing us from doing things we should. The late-night snacker knows it's not healthy to eat before bedtime—but what's the harm in a little snack? Eventually, however, the scale glares disapproval with its growing numbers. The snacker looks around as he's poised on the scale, hoping someone else's foot is pressed on it. But the only feet he finds are his own.

Why do we start habits anyway? Our son was fourteen when he started smoking. His father and I tried to persuade him to stop before it became an addictive habit. We warned him that he'd eventually want to quit, and he would find it an enormous struggle. "So why start?" we pleaded. After ten years of smoking, he learned a hard lesson when he tried to quit.

What's the lesson here? Don't start a bad habit. It will become a beast that can rob you of your joy, entrap you, and keep you from living the healthy, balanced life you desire. The problem is, we often start habits unknowingly. If you've allowed certain habits to drag you down, don't worry. Despite their strength, negative habits *can* be defeated.

Lifecycle and Strength of a Habit

Something nags in your stomach. It's a craving to eat something—anything! You look at the clock. Sure enough, your body knows it's the late hour. Time to feed. The nagging and the late hour are stimuli that awaken the pangs in your stomach—and move you to action. Your feet hit the floor. You head to the fridge, cupboard, pantry—anywhere there's food.

Every time you're stimulated, you repeat the action. This is the birthing of a habit. When we repeat a habit, we reinforce it and make it stronger.

Stimulus is like a glue that keeps us attached to a habit. It makes us dependent upon it by creating a zone of comfort for us. Unfortunately, comfort promotes undesired behavior. Be that as it may, comfort is comfort, and many of us keep giving in to the vicious circle.

Have you wondered why some habits are easier to break than others? Experts say it's based upon repeated stimulus and response. If a certain stimulus produces a uniform response, it's more likely to become a habit than if it produces a variety of different responses. Therefore, a consistent stimulus creates a consistent response.

If the response is rewarding, it is even more likely that the habit will be engrained in our behavior. This is the entrapment of habits: we are conditioned toward a certain behavior because we find benefit in it. Every time the late-night snacker savors his tasty treat, he reinforces the habit to eat the next night, the night after, and so on.

The more we reinforce a habit, the deeper it becomes etched in our memory. Stimulus triggers memory, and when we give in, we deepen the strength of the memory.

Defeating a Habit

So how can we dilute habit strength? Well, the simple answer is to stop repeating the behavior. But since we didn't create our habit overnight, we can't expect to stop our behavior overnight. We desire instant change: we want to get thinner *now*; stop smoking *now*; cool down our hot tempers *now*. But life works best when we are patient and create time and space for change to occur.

At an interpersonal communication seminar I was teaching, Margareta asked me how she should communicate with her adult son. He hung around her house all day and refused to work or attend college. I asked how long he'd been behaving like this. The corners of her mouth tightened before she responded. "It seems forever," she said. "Maybe a couple years. I can't get him to do anything since he graduated from high school. He says he's miserable and that if he could get a job he would. But honestly," she glanced down at her tightly bound-together hands, "he doesn't even look for work."

I suggested that *she* could be the key factor in increasing her son's habit strength—and her own. Her habit of allowing him to hang around the house had to stop. Once she controlled *her* behavior, then his behavior could no longer be reinforced.

Six months later Margareta sent me an e-mail announcing that she had taken a stand and laid out a list of daily chores for her son. It had taken time, but eventually her son had broken his laziness habit. Ultimately he found a full-time job and started taking an evening college course.

In the 1960s TV show *Bewitched* starring Elizabeth Montgomery, Samantha Stephens, a witch married to an ordinary man, couldn't resist using her magical powers to solve problems. She cleverly wiggled her nose, and poof, problem solved! Wouldn't it be wild if we could change our lives by twitching our noses? But since this option is a fantasy made in Hollywood, let's look at some tips to reset a good attitude and break the stronghold of our beast.

Make a Plan

Once we have decided to tame the beast, we need to put our commitment to a plan. Before we do anything, we need to consider what we're really trying to accomplish and how we'll chart our progress. In other words, we should write down the habit we want to break, how we'll accomplish it, and a reasonable timeframe to reach our goal.

Many people set seasonal deadlines to accomplish their goals. For instance, someone might want to be able to wear a new bathing suit on the first day of summer. Some people want to lose a few pounds before the holidays in order to enjoy guilt-free holiday cheer. What about the class reunion? We want to look amazing to our old high-school friends, so we set a timeframe to fit (or squeeze) into that alluring smaller dress or belt size.

It's also a good idea to incorporate a schedule of rewards for meeting milestones in our goals. Rewards keep us focused and motivated to improve our lives. They give us something to look forward to after we have invested discipline into our lives. Please don't deprive yourself of this important benefit.

It's important for us to recognize that our self-determination will ebb and flow as we carry out our plans. But we will also find that self-discipline will play a huge role as to how well we travel. Even the best-laid plans can become a pile of what ifs should we lose our focus.

If we do lose our focus, however, we shouldn't be hard on ourselves. We simply need to dust ourselves off and pick up our plan where we left off, remembering how important our goals were to us when we first made a commitment to change.

Change Your Belief System

Belief systems are the stories we tell ourselves to define our personal views on values, norms, and beliefs. A belief system establishes truth as we see it; it is the foundation on which we stand. That foundation shapes our perception and our sense of reality, and this reality helps us make common sense of the world around us.

A belief system has the power to propel us to achieve the unbelievable, or it can also paralyze our desire and determination for a better life. It will influence how we view a situation and help us develop good coping skills.

If we have trouble breaking down the beast of bad habits in our lives, then we need to change our belief system. Here are a few suggestions to help bring about success:

1. Come to terms with the bad habit.
2. Recognize the severity of the problem.
3. Believe that you can do something about the problem.
4. Define your motivation and values.

5. Define your reward. You'll want to be sure it's a reward that promotes good behavior.

I have found that the key to strengthening a new belief system requires a long-term commitment to one's goals. I have also learned that the process of building a new belief system does not happen quickly, especially if the repeated pattern has been part of a person's life for a long time.

I held a certain belief system when suffering with a beast for many years—the beast of anorexia. Experts say that eating disorders are mental illnesses, but by the grace of God, I was able to work my way through this disease by creating a new belief system. I also discovered that with each step I took to demolish my dysfunction, I couldn't wiggle my nose and have the problem instantly solved! It was a step-by-step process.

I became an anorexic shortly after I married a man who had three sons. I had a daughter. Let's do the math—I had an instant family of four children ranging in age from three to six years! I honestly thought I could handle my new life, but the gigantic demands of work and a blended family made me feel inadequate—as if I wasn't enough. My emotions were frayed at the ends because of the first lie I told myself: you have to be a supermom.

The second lie I told myself was that it was okay to control food, and I embarked upon a destructive path to control my food and my weight. I developed eating rituals to ensure control over these areas of my life. When eating out with friends, I'd peruse the menu and talk about the different entrees as though each one was the most delicious item on the menu. After all the buildup, I'd order a side of broccoli—hold the cheese, please. Other times I'd order a full entrée, eat a few bites, and play with the rest—moving food from one side of the plate to the other with my fork. After every meal I fantasized about the next one. When the next meal finally came, I couldn't wait to eat, but after a few bites I stopped eating.

My reality—my belief system—told me that I was never thin enough. A size 2 wasn't small enough. So I developed a strict exercise schedule. I ran eight miles a day, six days per week. Rain or shine, I was out pounding the pavement. I ran before work, during lunch, after work. When running started to take a toll on my body, I got into jazzercise.

The exercise regime was manic as well. The more I exercised, the more I needed more. The high from released endorphins that experts talk about, although good for motivation and ambition, was also a source of angst. I could never sit still. I always had to be doing something, anything, to keep up with the endorphins that had fired up my body. I could never find a place of rest, a place to enjoy life.

But one day my world changed.

When I became pregnant with our son, I realized that I could no longer starve myself. If nothing else, I had to eat for my baby. Since I was eating for my child, I lost the guilt I'd had in eating for myself. I was able to enjoy food and not control it. I experienced a sense of wellness after I ate. I felt strong and had more energy. The tension that had haunted me for controlling every bite of food was gone. I was finally free to relax and enjoy living. I laughed more.

I realized that feeding my body (for my baby) allowed me to experience the old me—the one not driven to obsession. The anorexic me had worked hard to keep my body looking super thin even though people had said I looked like a prisoner in a refugee camp. Deep down inside I had wanted the old me back, but before now I hadn't known how to find her.

After I had nursed my son for nearly a year, thoughts of food began haunting me again. But I refused to cave in, because I finally felt terrific with guilt-free eating. I liked myself now, which helped me to accept myself.

God never intended me to be controlled by food and exercise. Rather, his plan for me was to live an abundant life, helping others, making a positive impact in my world. I couldn't do that while being held captive by the life of an anorexic. When I was anorexic, life was all about me and no one else. Changing my belief system meant realizing that the world no longer revolved around me. I had a family to care for—they had to come first. They needed me to be healthy and not look like a skeleton wearing a dress and high heels. By changing my belief system, I was able to overcome and stay free of anorexia.

Identify the Source of a Habit

Unfortunately, the new belief system I had started during my pregnancy with our son worked only until the next catastrophe. While recovering from anorexia, I began to see a pattern in my disease: during stressful events I fell into the old pattern of trying to control food and maintain a grueling exercise program.

One particular event in my life kept me falling off my wagon: our youngest son, at fourteen, began running away from home. This was a recurring event for a stretch of some four agonizing years. Anorexia massacred my life once again. I shrunk from a size 4 to a 0.

But one day my world turned in an unexpected positive direction again.

Our son stopped running away. We began attending weekly counseling sessions and monthly meetings with his homeroom teacher. God was slowly putting the broken pieces of our lives back together again.

One day during this season of healing, as I took down Christmas decorations, strangely, I felt hungry. This was a shocking experience, because anorexics tell themselves they're *never* hungry. But this day I actually was. I took a slice of cheese out of the refrigerator and ate it. The protein instantly made me feel better. I continued taking down the Christmas decorations and experienced hunger throughout the day, and each time, I ate protein or drank a glass of orange juice. I felt strong and energetic. The pent-up tension from not allowing myself to eat slowly faded away. I started feeling like a brand-new person—just as I had when I had allowed myself to eat when I was pregnant with our son.

I hope you don't think I'm off my rocker, but while experiencing this new sensation that day, I heard a voice as clearly as if I had been speaking with someone else say, "Enough!" I stared at a half-naked Christmas tree, knowing in the core of my being that God was rescuing me. He was saying that I'd had enough of the bondage. Enough of fighting to control. Enough of my world being all about me in pieces. Enough!

For many months I pondered this command "Enough." Deep down I'd known for a long time that I'd had enough, but now I felt as if God had also had enough of watching me live a life of entrapment.

His command helped me to put together a new belief system. It made me stronger, devoted to healing, and more motivated than the system I had adopted during my pregnancy. I learned that in order to release the grip of anorexia—although a disease, I had created a habit of not eating—I had to identify how I had gotten to be an anorexic. To search out this dilemma, I asked myself a probing question: "What got me here?"

As I worked through my history with this disease, I found clues that helped me see the root causes of my struggle and blast my routine to pieces: feelings of inadequacy, believing that I was not good enough, keeping up a façade of perfectionism, always needing to be in control of every situation and everyone else. These clues were part of the process of discovering the root cause of my habit.

As I mentioned earlier, whenever my world became too stressful, I fell into a belief system that said I had to control my food. I now learned to take a stand, however, and I drew from my "enough" belief system and told myself, "*Stop!*" Whenever I heard the slippery voice of anorexia taunting me to control the uncontrollable, I responded, "There's no more room for anorexia in my life. I'm healed. I'm healthy. I'm emotionally stronger. Go away!" These pledges, as I call them, added fuel to my "enough" belief system.

All of us, from time to time, can get knee deep into a habit before realizing that we're trapped. If you've experienced this, take a few minutes and ask yourself, "What got me here?"

Break the Lifecycle of a Habit

The unexpected truth about living with a bad habit is that we create a comfort zone around it. We may be unhappy in it, but we are cushioned by its comfort—and that comfort keeps us bound to it.

As a child, I had to sit next to my mom whenever we visited her friends. Other kids ran around, laughing and chasing each other, but I was glued to my mother's side. Once the hostess invited me to play. I started to stand, but my mother grabbed my arm and pulled me back to her side. She smiled to her friend and said, "Oh no, Carol needs to learn that when she's in other people's homes, she can't have the run of their house."

While in high school, I began attending parties, and I hugged a corner of the room as though chained to my mother's side. But after some persuading from friends, I began to venture out of my comfort zone. Each time I did, I broke the cycle of that habit.

I learned, when I had the urge to repeat a habit, to *stop*! Instead of feeding the habit, I made a concerted effort to step out of my comfort zone. The more we step outside this illusionary feeling of comfort, the quicker we step into freedom.

Employ Time and Disuse

Employing time and disuse regarding our bad habits is another version of the well-known use-it-or-lose-it concept. Disuse of a behavior causes that behavior to be forgotten. Over time, efforts to break a learned behavior can be accomplished if we stop practicing a habit. Something exciting happens to our brains when we don't repeat a habit: we actually reshape our brain. Soon the brain will forget the pattern, and eventually the habit's impact will be lessened. We weaken the beast by simply forgetting it.

My grandmother taught me to speak Japanese. I spoke it fluently, but when my mother remarried and we moved away from my grandmother, I began to lose the language over time as my visits with her became less and less frequent. I simply forgot certain words. Although I wish I could have practiced my native language more and was sad at its loss, this is a good illustration about not repeating a behavior and therefore forgetting it altogether.

I've learned the importance of the use-it-or-lose-it concept. It made my journey to break a habit easier, because the less I repeated the habit, the more my brain got one step closer to forgetting it, and the sooner I broke the stronghold of a beast. I soon adopted a phrase that became my affirmation: "Don't repeat! Forget it! Defeat it!"

Echo Your Thoughts

When my mother, grandmother, and I first moved to the mainland from Hawaii, we lived in a multistory building. The stairway and hallways were made of dark mahogany wood. The ceilings were very high. Thin curtains covered mahogany-framed windows. The floors were planked with dark hardwood. Everything was dark. And everything, to my four-year-old imagination, made my new home seem spooky. The noise of our footsteps and the voices that oozed from nowhere were strange to me, but my mother told me that these creepy sounds were echoes. They were like a shadow that followed me everywhere, repeating their eerie chant.

Echoing, in a psychological sense, is a process of rehearsing words and thoughts. Echoing feeds thoughts, and eventually thoughts form behavior. That's why echoing is a major player in breaking a habit. First our echo needs to be positive. For example, when we don't give in to a habit, we can echo, "I won! I won! I won!" The process of echoing reinforces the behavior we want to see in ourselves. Thus echoing reprograms the brain to encourage change. The power of upbeat and encouraging words helps ignite our determination and unleashes us from slavery to that nagging beast.

Our son tried unsuccessfully to stop smoking time and again while in his late twenties. But one day, during a triumph, he called me. His voice chimed over the phone, "Hey, Mom! I haven't lit up in four days!" He was echoing his new behavior. It's now been over five years, and he hasn't lit up! Way to go, son!

Another term for echoing is "self-talk." Typically this is a one-sided conversation in which our minds tell us how we should live. If we're not careful, we can fill our minds with negative words, which is the standard language for most self-talk. But we should practice considerate self-talk. When negativity dominates our minds, we can hit our mute button and sternly tell ourselves, "Stop echoing right now! I'm working hard to break this habit. I don't need any pessimistic interference!"

Flip That Thought

We can't control what pops into our mind, but we can control what we do with our thoughts. Whenever negative thoughts enter our minds, we should think of a thought that's the direct opposite. In other words, we can flip that negative thought and discover positive change in our goal trajectory.

Char had tried every diet invented. But try as she might, most were a failure. I asked her to talk about the hardest experience she'd had with each diet. She thought for a moment, then her eyes popped with surprise. "You know," she exclaimed, "every time I start a new diet, I tell myself, 'You failed before.'" After explaining to Char how to flip that negative thought, she gave it a try. Her flipped thought was, "This is a new diet. A new start to a new me!" I saw her a few months later, and she was a dress size smaller. The first thing she said to me as she spun around was, "I flipped my thought! Look how great that worked!" High five to Char!

Conclusion

Bad habits are a trap not only for us but also for others within our influence. Habits can become masters of our lives and cause us to become whatever we give in to. Not only that, but they prevent us from getting to the next level of growth in our lives.

I didn't realize I had an eating disorder until many years after it began, when I felt entrapped by a strict eating and exercise regime. By the time I realized I had a problem, the anorexia had sunk its claws into my behavior. If I could have understood how obsessive I would become over food, I would never have started starving myself. In the end my behavior only complicated my need to control, and that was no way to live.

We often embark upon a habit innocently and unknowingly. But blaming our circumstances or even blaming the devil won't change our behavior, our attitude, or our self-esteem. We must break the bond of habit strength, own who we have become because of our bad habits, and step out in faith to change.

Fortunately, our brains are willing to be reprogrammed. All we need is a plan—a course of action to progressively and deliberately wipe out the bad habit so that we can forget it and create a new belief system that justifies the change in our behavior.

Corrie ten Boom, a Dutch Christian who, along with her father and other family members, helped many Jews escape the Nazi Holocaust during World War II, explained faith in a unique way: "It is not my ability, but my response to God's ability, that counts."[1] Grab on to the hand of divine rescue, and allow God's supremacy to shatter the beast hidden deep in a habit.

Action Points

Perhaps you have been entrapped in a bad habit for years. How can you change something that is so entrenched in your life?

Attitude is a major factor in breaking the stronghold of bad habits. The pressure to change can seem defeating. Some days you may find that you've taken a few steps backward. But don't be discouraged. Back up and find the place where you slipped, then start from that point and begin marching on your trail with new insight and determination.

The truth is, you can break habit strength, but it takes work and determination. The following questions are designed to help you analyze your habits and create a plan to change—to leave bad habits behind and to welcome and thrive in brand-new habits!

What habit would you like to change?

When are you most likely to repeat a bad habit? (For example, many people who smoke enjoy a light-up after a meal.)

When your inner clock reminds you that it's time to repeat a bad habit, what can you do to offset the strength of that habit? (For example, a smoker may chew a piece of gum after dinner instead of lighting up.)

It's important to start any change with a plan. It should consist of what you want to accomplish. Write down what you desire to accomplish and then write out how you'll chart your progress.

Part of breaking a habit is changing your belief system. Regarding the habit you listed in the first question, write out what needs to change in your belief system.

Here's an important tip: if you can identify the cause or source of your habit, give it a name; then you're that much closer to breaking the unwanted habit. Take a few minutes to identify the source of a habit you want to break.

What echoing, or self-talk, could you say to yourself to encourage yourself to stick with your efforts to break a habit?

Whenever you try to make any change in your life, your mind tends to fight back. It gets lazy and doesn't want to work hard. When negative thoughts pop into your mind, how can you control them? How would you change a nagging negative thought into a positive one?

8

Reengineering Your Life—Exchanging Bad Habits for Good

*It is time for us to stand and cheer for the doer, the achiever,
the one who recognizes the challenge and does something about it.*

VINCE LOMBARDI

I was in my early twenties when I read my first self-help book. It was during this time that I finally began to feel grounded, secure, and hopeful. I had come out of a divorce and the death of my newborn, and I was raising my toddler. The author challenged readers to live on the edge, daring people to live large, love large, and prosper large in the promises of God.

At this stage in my life, I wasn't ready to live or prosper large, but I was ready to love and be loved. I hungered to learn more of

God's limitless love, his total acceptance of me, and his healing power to ransom my hopelessness and turn my mourning into utter joy. Love, I believed, was the panacea to all the pain, misunderstanding, and emptiness that had hovered over me like an animus cloud.

I had a drive, something deep inside me that needed, wanted, to base my entire life on love—to give myself away to a deep level of contentment. A few times in my young life I had loved, and it had brought me a great sense of completeness. I wanted that again. Little did I understand that I was on a quest to reengineer my life—to replace my bad habits with new, good ones. Back then it wasn't called reengineering or reinventing or rebooting; it was just called turning over a new leaf. But I was ready!

I looked for love in all kinds of places. Sometimes I found it in wrong places—in men who didn't have my best intentions in mind. But I must say that while discovering ways to reengineer myself in love, God protected me and kept me on the path of breakthrough and safety. In his love I felt a kind of joy unspeakable, and this quality of unconditional love carved out my journey. Along my travel I learned that God's love is an incredible force, and I instinctively knew when I had stepped outside of it—the emptiness returned. So I saddled myself with his love.

At this stage of my life, I was just venturing into a world that made high demands of me. My first priority was to support my daughter—to find a job and get off welfare. At the time I wasn't aware of the importance of breaking bad habits; I just wanted to love. But my strong desire automatically directed me to get rid of all the junk in my life that could interfere with my quest to find love.

Before I could put my full weight into this adventure of reengineering, I had to make room in my heart for love—to get rid of things that should never have been part of my life. Loving and carrying around junk could no longer coexist. As I let go of poisonous character traits that would jeopardize the success of my journey—jealousy, distrust, control, anger—I would then have room to fill my life with something else. I turned to God and told him that I believed that love had the power to cast out the ugly toxic behaviors in my life.

Reengineering Happens in Seasons

Have you ever watched the growth and development of a baby's motor skills? It's fascinating to watch a bundle of joy grow through different phases. The baby learns to raise its head, then its shoulders, then to sit up, crawl, and walk—or some jet-setter babies bypass walking and take off running. Seasons of growth aren't limited to babies; in fact, there is a season for everything under the sun, and that includes reengineering our lives. One season of new growth creates a foundation for the next season to come.

In my early twenties I learned the invaluable concept of love, and this reengineered my life by teaching me self-acceptance and helping me become brave enough to share my love with others. In my late twenties anorexia came knocking at my door, and loving myself became a challenge. I found then that the foundational power of love from an earlier season became the cornerstone of loving myself and helped me control the spiraling effect of self-loathing as I stood at the precipice of physical and mental destruction.

One day my adult daughter (the toddler I had raised alone as a young adult) and I were talking about my efforts to overcome anorexia. She made an observation that knocked me off my chair: "Mom, I watched your eating habits as a teenager and wanted to be just like you. But you wouldn't let me skip meals like you did, and now I'm so grateful. You lived on the edge of disaster in your own life, but somehow you knew there was a line you couldn't cross." I leaned back into my chair and was overwhelmingly thankful that the season of reengineering in my early twenties had been my lifesaver for the later season in rebooting my life. It was my daughter's lifesaver as well.

The Space that Habit Once Occupied

What happens to the space that's left within us once we break a habit? If we don't fill the empty space with good behavior, we leave an opening for that bad habit to sneak back in. Since we've worked so hard to get rid of the habit, we should be willing to work even harder to make sure it doesn't return. In chapter 2 we discussed choosing to exercise personal-quality DNA with the picture of an angel sitting on one shoulder and a devil on the other. This idea of good and bad are two primary drivers we face on a daily basis. By seeking the good, we can stop the growth of bad behavior.

After we have successfully broken a habit, our work is not done. The truth is, it has just begun. We need to continually assess what is good and what is bad about the life we want to live. Remember, our bad habits are always looking for ways to get back into our lives. Let's put an end to the slippery practices that try to fill the empty space our bad behavior once called home.

One key to successfully filling up the vacuum of a bad habit is finding something better and replacing the bad habit with a good one. If you habitually run to the kitchen and rummage through the goodie drawer—that precious stash of cookies, candies, donuts, and honey-covered nuts—head for the front door instead. Go outside and take a leisurely walk—get that inner wiggle out of you. When you come back, stay busy, and most importantly, stay out of the kitchen!

When my daughter was a toddler and attracted to all kinds of mischief, I'd remove a forbidden thing and then scold her. One day my grandmother saw how poorly I was training her great-granddaughter, and she offered a suggestion: "Give her something else to play with. It'll replace the mischief." I did, and it worked! That's what we need to do with a bad habit. In other words, we need to replace the vacuum that the bad habit has left. If we don't, our negative attitudes won't go away.

Two Attitudes that Make or Break Reengineering Efforts

We are driven by two kinds of attitudes that I call "flippant" and "earnest." Flippancy is the obnoxious one. It produces anger, jealousy, unforgiveness, pride, and laziness. These character traits can create fear, and fear can hold us back, causing us to become flippant in our efforts to improve our lives.

The other attitude, earnestness, is pleasant, good, patient, forgiving. It produces love, kindness, humility, and self-control. By comparison, earnestness is shown by our strengths, while our weaknesses are displayed by flippancy.

These two attitudes are continually fighting against each other, but only one of them will win. It all depends on which attitude we choose to feed. The more we feed a certain one, the faster it will grow. The next time you're tempted to feed a habit, ask, "Do I really want this habit to grow? Or do I want to starve it and step up higher to achieve my goal?" You can also ask yourself, "Do I want to see flippant attributes of anger, jealousy, bitterness, pride and laziness in my life, or is earnestness, which causes fruits of love, harmony, peace, and contentment to abound, a better choice?"

We were created with earnest strength attributes of love, kindness, humility, patience, self-control, and other good qualities. These make up our personal-quality DNA that God has prescribed in all of us. When we exercise this DNA, we behave the way we were meant to. When we live the way we were meant to, the earnest driver cuts through our flippant habits, and we end up with true happiness. When true happiness abounds, we have the right driver that will help plot our course toward a balanced life.

In order to develop good habits—that is, an attitude of earnestness—we first need to choose to feed the right attitude. Let's look at a few ideas that can help direct our paths to feed, nurture, and blossom earnestness. In fact, the stronger our earnest attitude, the easier it is to reengineer our lives.

Start Small

An old Chinese proverb conveys the logic and reasonableness of starting small: "It is better to take many small steps in the right direction than to make a great leap forward only to stumble backward." When we start small in our efforts to feed the good and starve the bad, we find that our life experiences will act as a foundation to springboard us in the right direction. Lessons from past experiences will also encourage us to keep hopeful in our efforts, stay focused, and remain on task. We'll get further by taking small steps than by taking one big leap.

It's not pleasant when a person bites off more than he can chew. Taken literally, it's bad manners to stuff our faces and talk with food in our mouths; but figuratively speaking, this is exactly what we do in our fast-paced world, perhaps because we feel that we have little choice but to jump into a plan that's too big for us. But do we?

One of my flippant-attitude habits is to go like ninety—to take big leaps and finish things early. Whether I'm doing an aerobic exercise program, practicing yoga, engaging in a work project, kayaking, or hiking, I drive myself to the edge of exhaustion and then complain because I'm plumb worn out. It finally dawned on me that if I'm tired, I'm no good to anyone, especially myself. So I made a choice to start small. For example, instead of working eight to ten hours straight, head buried in piles of research, I set a timer for two hours. When it chimed, I took a ten-minute break. Then I set the timer again for another two hours. I paced myself—started small.

Once I created a two-hour habit, it was time to increase it. Again, still starting small, I stretched the next time limit to three hours. I eventually tried to work for four hours but found that a three-hour period with a ten-minute break was the best plan for me.

As I continued to feed earnestness, I discovered that going ninety is for superwomen, and the last time I checked, a cape and tights weren't part of my work attire. The result: I am no longer stupefied, glassy eyed, and brain frozen at the end of the day.

Stay Dependable

As we work to reengineer our lives and replace our old habits with good ones, we not only need to start small, but we also need to rely upon ourselves to reach our goals. For example, when we get hungry, we rely on our legs to enable us to walk to the kitchen and our hands to help us prepare something delicious. But if our legs refuse to carry us to the kitchen and our hands won't put a meal together, then, well, we'll starve. When we are hungry, we need to know that we will be fed. When we are trying to develop good habits, we need to depend on ourselves to stay on the path, to keep feeding earnestness.

We also need to trust in ourselves to know that we'll stick with our plan to develop and feed good habits. Doing sit-ups each day for a week as we try to get back in shape then forgetting for two weeks and then starting again for one more week before we forget again is not likely to help us out. With this start-stop-start-stop method, any progress we make developing new habits and improving our fitness quickly disappears.

The key to breaking bad habits is to work smarter, not harder. Let's face it—changing habits is no easy feat. But by working smarter, we can improve our journeys by staying dependable.

Keep Moving Forward

At some point every effort hits a plateau. Let's say your goal is to lose twenty pounds. You shed fifteen and can't lose any more. You decide to starve yourself, do more workouts, but still no results—ugh! You've hit a wall. Should you give up? Please don't! Keep focused on your goal, and keep working hard. Never ever give up. Keep running your race. Keep feeding earnestness. Keep doing your best. Then prepare to be amazed, because your body will react to the consistent hard work—and the pounds will drop.

Something exciting happens when we keep our eyes on the prize and keep moving forward. We become unstuck, and our new behavior moves in a forward direction. Here's the key: when we move forward, we leave our past. This means no looking back or falling backward. We can't move forward if we are constantly looking back. Moving forward gives us a second chance. We need to declare that our past is over. Our forward direction is brand new, and if our direction is brand new, then we become brand new. We have reengineered our attitude and behavior. Nothing in our lives is the same—that is, if we choose to keep moving forward.

Celebrate moving forward by moving forward! Every step forward teaches us to recognize new possibilities in our lives. These possibilities will turn into opportunities, and opportunities will turn into great stories of success.

The Happiness Surround

We especially need positive, supportive, and happy people in our circle when we're growing good habits. Sometimes well-intentioned people say negative things to us, and we need to let them know that the solution to our success is their support, laughter, and encouragement. Make a list of people who are positive and will support your goal. Stay in touch with them, and enjoy the power of the "happiness surround."

Marcel Proust, a French intellectual, author, and critic best known for his seven-volume novel *In Search of Lost Time*, said, "Let us be grateful to people who make us happy; they are the charming gardeners who make our souls blossom."[1]

A Scoop of Double-Chocolate Peanut-Butter-Cup Ice Cream, Please!

Years ago when I attended college at night, worked full time, and took care of my family, one of my professors asked how I managed to accomplish all my responsibilities. "A scoop of ice cream, please," I told him. I explained that I made a monthly trip to my favorite ice-cream parlor for a scoop of double-chocolate peanut-butter-cup ice cream. It was my reward for juggling a busy and demanding schedule.

Remember, earnestness needs to have rewards. You might want to make a weekly assessment of your progress, and when you do well, give yourself a reward. This frequent assessment will help you keep a close watch on your journey and even help you find your way back if you unintentionally take a wrong turn.

Conclusion

We all struggle with pesky annoyances that can keep us in a flippant attitude. Be patient and kind to yourself. The more we feed and nurture a good habit, the more it becomes part of our lifestyles. Keep fighting the good fight. Never give up on a new habit, because if you do, you'll be giving up on yourself.

God is always on our side. He looks for ways to help us get better. He sees the bad habits we do to ourselves that rob us of our joy and cause us to live half full. God certainly doesn't want us to live in bondage. His primary goal is to set us free. He wants us to enjoy life to its fullest and aspire to levels we could never see ourselves reaching. Never feel that you're alone in reaching for your goals. God sees so much more than we do, and through all our efforts to replace bad habits with good ones, he promises never to give up on us. If God is on our side, we can ask, "What power does a pesky habit have over me?"

Action Points

You have the awesome privilege of running your own race. You're not responsible for anyone else's race—just your own. Examine these action points to help you commit to reengineering your life.

Why is starting small important?

You've developed a plan to break a habit. Is there a good habit that you can replace the bad one with? What is it?

It's important to surround yourself with people who will help you move forward. Make a list of some people who can help you in this.

What is your personal message to the attitudes of flippancy and earnestness?

What kind of reward would you give yourself for standing tall against bad habits? This could be a weekly reward or one you give yourself each time you accomplish some small step toward your goal.

_____
_____
_____
_____

9

Dealing with Unexpected Change

We must always change, renew, rejuvenate ourselves; otherwise we harden.

JOHANN WOLFGANG VON GOETHE

Dear Mom and Dad,
   I can't live here anymore. You guys are good parents, but I have problems and need to figure them out for myself. Don't worry about me. I'm living with a good family who goes to church. I love you.

Our son was barely fourteen the first time he ran away. My world turned upside down. Every word in his note sliced through my soul. My mind raced. "I have problems." Why didn't he want our help? "Don't worry about me." I knew he was guarding our feelings, but why was he running? "I'm living with a good family who goes to church." He knew that family and church were important values to us, but why had he gone to someone else? Why? Why?

When our lives are turned upside down, it is easy for us to ask "How could this have happened?" as we desperately search for answers that make sense. The harsh truth is that there aren't any easy remedies for cancer, death, the skeletal frame of a once-robust loved one, a runaway child. When we're emotionally invested in someone or something, it's not as simple as taking two aspirin and waiting thirty minutes to feel better. Instead, we ache in places we didn't know we had, and try as we might, it's hard to pinpoint the source of the indescribable pain that tunnels itself deep inside. When the unexpected happens, how do we get back to a place that makes sense?

I asked this question a hundred times when our son was AWOL. I learned that regardless of the degree of my pain, I needed to understand the source of my angst. As I searched my anguished heart, I finally discovered what was really bothering me: unexpected change.

Change bamboozles its way into our lives through the unexpected, the unwanted, the unsolicited. We can run from it, but, as the old saying goes, we can't hide. If we could put our hurt, fear, and angst aside, we would be better prepared to tackle problems objectively. But the truth is, in the midst of unexpected change, we're smothered with high emotion, which leads to subjective thinking. The danger of a subjective mind-set is that it leads us to believe that we're going in the right direction even while we're aimlessly firing bullets of fear into a dark senseless space.

When our son ran away, this huge change disrupted our lives. We were fearful for our son's safety and worried about his struggle and unhappiness that had forced him to run. We were shaken out of our secure and routine home life. My husband and I tried to go about living normally, but our son had left a place in our family that only he could fill, and the void he left was as big as the east is from the west.

Nighttime was dreadful. I'd lie in bed, wondering. Wondering if our son was safely sleeping on a bed or out in a back alley curled under a bush. My heart broke into a million jagged pieces, each one crying out, "Will I ever see my son again?" Some mornings it was impossible for me to get out of bed. But in those days I realized something very important: in my darkest hour, God was with me.

As I lay in bed, crying my heart dry, he was there. When I was in the shower, sobbing against the pounding water drops, he was there. When I stared into nothing at the dinner table, moving the tasteless food across my plate, he was there. There wasn't a place I went that God wasn't present. Just as in the well-known poem *Footprints*, in which only one set of footprints appeared in the sand as God carried the overburdened person, I too was carried. This heavenly support allowed me to have good days—days when I could make sense of my thoughts, even though my predicament was nonsensical.

It was during one of these good days that I learned an important lesson that brought me comfort in the midst of my change: even though I felt bamboozled, frightened, confused, smothered, I needed to *step back*. Yes, step back. Sometimes when we're stuck in pain and disbelief, we feel as though our intense pain and disappointment need a huge solution, but the toughest of times calls for the simplest fix, because that's about all we can handle. When I stepped back, I began finding ways to work with the change in my life—and to grow through it in my quest toward an abundant life.

If you're facing adversity of any size, try allowing space between you and your challenge. This will give you a better view of your situation and help you find the strength and flexibility you need to walk victoriously through the unwelcome circumstances in your life.

You Have What It Takes to Stand Strong

As we grapple with painful change in our lives, we have a powerful ally—one that has already prepared us for the unwelcome change. It's called past experience. When we are blindsided by change, God makes sure that we have had enough experiences to help us stand strong.

Each event we experience prepares us for the next challenge. It equips us, makes us ready, and sets us up for success. You may say, "I'm not equipped, ready, or set up. A peaceful, balanced life is a pie-in-the-sky, unattainable dream." But I would say, "Put your full weight into your history. It is the foundation to guide and support you all the way to the next level. Even if you don't feel ready, you are. Don't be afraid. Life experience has your back!"

If you're still not sure about this concept, search your past. Reunite with the experiences that have brought you up to your current challenge. Events in our lives aren't happenstance. They have a purpose, even those that are as simple as a conversation with someone who has lived what you're now living.

I wish I could tell you that our son never ran away again, but he did—many times. The disappointment and despair were worse each time he ran. As a family, we had worked so hard—counseling, conducting health chats, listening to each other—how could we have failed?

When my husband and I had married, we'd had four children in tow from previous relationships; surely these kids would have been the hardest to raise. But these four never ran away, shoplifted, posted graffiti, or were incarcerated. Why couldn't we raise this fifth child who had been raised with two loving parents? After all, he hadn't suffered the confusion of divorce as his sister and brothers had. What was suddenly wrong with our parenting skills? I just couldn't figure this out.

I began to see, however, that each runaway event was a learning tool for me, a life experience, a building block. Instead of crumbling with heartache and disappointment, I needed to stay resilient and not interpret my son's choices as my failure.

Tame That Fear

Fear is a learned behavior. We've learned it either from other people or our own experience. For example, I'm deathly afraid of spiders.

Too many skinny legs. Each leg can mean trouble. I'm not quite sure where I learned to be fearful of these crawly creatures, but I did, and I passed that fear to our son.

When he was a toddler, our family lived in the country, where colonies of spiders cohabitated with us. One day my son and I went for a walk down our country lane, and there on the road we came across a two-thousand-pound tarantula. Okay, maybe it was not two thousand pounds, but fear had me seeing it that big. I screamed and scooped up my son, telling him never to touch spiders—you never knew what all their legs would do to you. From the time he was a toddler until now, as a grown man in his thirties, my son has been dreadfully afraid of spiders. Fear, whether learned or experienced, is powerful. It can keep us stuck. Try as we might to move forward, fear holds us back with its paralyzing grip.

You may be like so many people who carry the burden of fear. Isn't it time to let the paralysis go? Get unstuck. Have the courage to overcome. The next time fear begins to well up in your being, stay strong, and follow this tip: step into fear. No, I'm not crazy. Here's what I mean: for me, stepping into fear means envisioning whatever I'm afraid of as a blob of green goop on the floor; then I take a deep breath and step right into the middle of that blob. This virtual experience allows me to face my fear, and when I do, it turns out that what I have feared is not as bad as I thought it was—or even something my mind has made up. By stepping into the fear, I realize there really wasn't anything to be afraid of. Try it—step into the fear. Many times fear is something we conjure up in our minds. Experts say that some fears are imaginary and therefore aren't fears in their truest sense. If we can tame our mind, we can tame our fear.

Part of our self-preservation technique is to anticipate a problem so that we can be prepared when it happens. This is a noteworthy effort, but when we allow fear to consume our lives, it becomes ineffective. We've all built fear monsters in our minds, but by facing our fear and standing tall, we can re-teach ourselves the necessary behaviors to tame fear.

The Sway Factor

What is broken can be fixed: broken hearts, broken dreams, broken ambitions. This same philosophy applies to the unwelcome challenges in our lives. If there is a positive found in an unwelcome challenge, it is this: every challenge opens a door to a solution, and one solution is found by way of something called the "sway factor."

Great bridges and skyscrapers endure storms because they sway slightly with the wind. Palm trees bend in tempestuous storms. All these are able to survive changes in weather due to their inherent sway factor. We too are equipped to do the same. For example, we instinctively know what to do when a cold has clogged our sinus passages; normally we adapt and breathe through our mouths. Yes, it's easy to flex when it comes to our physical condition, but it's tougher when change affects us mentally and emotionally. Let's take a closer look at the sway factor.

In order to sway during challenging times, we must be flexible and open minded. Flexibility helps us see change as an opportunity to make the most of situations we don't have power over. Becoming flexible gives us the capacity to be bent, usually without breaking. When we're flexible, we overcome our natural tendency to resist change. The first step in the sway process is to keep an open mind, and open mindedness leads to the next step: becoming adaptable by adjusting to different conditions.

But how in the world can we get in a groove for the sway factor?

Stretch Your Mind

When it comes to physical exercise, a good stretching routine will help a person avoid injury. Stretching allows flexibility in range of motion around specific joints. Stretching our minds actually broadens our frame of reference. Our minds are expanded to take in the necessary information that reshapes our attitude and helps us accept the things we cannot change.

That's what happened when our son kept running away. I had to stretch my mind to accept the truth: he was using drugs. The problem we were dealing with was the drug, not our son. When he spoke, the drugs were speaking. That was a gut-wrenching reality.

No parent says, "I want my baby to grow up to be a druggie. I look forward to the day he's incarcerated. I hope to find stolen merchandise in his room or discover tightly folded dollar bills from drug sales." When heartbreak shows up, our knee-jerk reaction is to close our minds in denial. But denial will keep our minds shut off from the truth.

It is beneficial for us to stretch our minds. The next time you find yourself in denial, *stop*! Even if the truth is painful, we're better off taking it all in and making an informed decision so that we can face the truth from an open mind. An open mind allows us to get the whole story, see the entire situation, and then make choices based upon a broader range of information.

Relinquish Stubbornness

Stubbornness is an entrenched resistance to change. It sees change as a threat, even if that change is positive and in our best interest. Sometimes we believe our only defense against change is to be stubborn. But is that the best choice?

It's easy to identify areas of stubbornness in our day-to-day lives, but how can we effectively resist this negative attitude when the rug is pulled out from beneath us? For me, each time our son ran, it was worse than the first time. The pain was insurmountable. But I had to focus on keeping myself whole for the time when our son would return home, because I believed he needed wholesome parents who could offer guidance and were not working from a place of pain and blame. In the midst of my heartache, I took a deep breath—a really deep breath—and then I took a step back. My pain was so big that it was tough for me to determine my attitude issues, but taking a breath and stepping back helped me identify my stubbornness. Not on my first attempt—to tell the truth, it took quite a few breaths and steps back. But my persistence paid off, and one day I was able to identify my stubbornness.

Deep inside I was holding on to how unfair my situation was. It was unfair that our son kept running away. It was unfair that I couldn't sleep, couldn't eat, couldn't be happy, couldn't, couldn't, couldn't. So I got rid of "couldn't" and searched for what I *could* do. I decided that I could pray more—pray for our son's safety and willingness to return home; pray for my marriage that was starting to splinter; pray for all kinds of desires and needs. You may find another remedy; whatever it is, make sure it keeps you in a forward-moving direction. Prayer did it for me—what might it be for you?

Do not fall into the pit so many people fall into. Often people don't take time to analyze the source of their stubbornness. They take an "oh well" attitude and accept the restrictive immobility of a stubborn mind-set. We've all dealt with a stubborn person. It wasn't the best experience, right? Stubbornness makes our thinking like a brick: hard, stiff, impenetrable. And really, who wants that?

So what is the source of stubbornness?

Stubbornness stems from ego. Ego interferes with our ability to become flexible. Why? Because ego has an extremely narrow view of a situation. It looks for the easiest way, the fastest way, the what's-in-it-for-me way. When we allow ego to dominate, we toss away flexibility. Ego is the culprit that rubs its hands, hopes we refuse to bend, then laughs as we break.

It's easy to become self-centered during any kind of challenging experience because we see the event through the lens of how it affects us. We tire of care giving; we wish we had time for ourselves. Our problem causes us to feel out of control in our lives. But the truth is, we should be more focused on the other people in our lives than on ourselves. Even if each of us is going through a health or financial situation by which we are directly affected, there are ways to shift from self-centeredness to being others-centered.

This is what a good friend of mine, Kathy, did when her cancer returned. She had been cancer free for five years, and on the day of her fifth anniversary, she decided to take the stairs at work instead of the elevator. Halfway up the stairs she found she could barely take the next step. Her breathing was labored. A few hours later her oncologist gave her the dreadful news: the cancer had returned. It was in her lungs and her brain.

Kathy did a lot of soul searching, and she decided how she was going to live through the remainder of her days. "Of all my sisters," she told me, "I wondered why I was the one who had come down with cancer. Why had it returned and given me only a few months to live? 'Why me?' I asked God. Then he answered—not in a clear voice but with a message deposited in my soul: 'Only you can handle the illness. Only you can show what it means to have faith—what it means to stay strong, to be resilient even in the darkness of death. Your life is a ministry to your family. No one can do what you're doing.'"

So what did Kathy do? She let go of self-centeredness and focused on her purpose: encouraging her family and friends with her trust in God. Her effort not only showed others how to remain resilient through challenges, but it also helped Kathy call upon her faith, which helped her to stay strong. Yes, she had some difficult days, but at her funeral her sisters told of her unyielding grace and overwhelming faith that had taught them lessons they possibly never would have realized.

Kathy was only forty-five when she passed away. At her funeral the church was packed to standing room only. Her daughter was pregnant with her first grandchild; her son had just gotten married. But Kathy had understood others-centeredness and given the beauty of who she was to so many people, even to those far beyond her reach.

Remove Resistance

There are two types of resistance, one positive and one negative:

- Defending our well-being
- Defying our well-being

When we *defend* our well-being, we resist temptation—craving food, overeating, or binging on junk food. This type of resistance is positive. *Defying* our well-being, on the other hand, is counterproductive.

When a change sneaks into our lives, we tend to defy it. We want life to remain as it was. We don't perceive that this change could bring about anything good. It could stretch us, strengthen our weakness, and take us to the next level. Still we resist it. We go against the new tide in our lives. When we do this, another layer of frustration compounds a difficult situation. This is why it is vital to let go of this kind of resistance that defies our well-being.

Once when I was knee deep in resistance, a thought stirred in my soul: *Go with the flow*. Having no other good options, I listened. Going with the flow helped me become flexible, and being flexible brought me back to a balanced state of being. Out went resistance, and in came flexibility—I was ready to fix things, not ditch them.

Out with the Old, In with the New

Holding on to old ideas and opinions simply because we are comfortable with them is a sign of inflexibility. This type of rigidity can keep us from achieving our goals toward living an abundant life. Rather than trying to control everything, we ought to try letting the process of life unfold in its own way and time. In this process there is a natural flow to the outcomes in our lives.

Why?

Because God has a plan and an answer for every life predicament. If inflexibility has us stuck, then we need to recognize that at the lowest place in our frustration, God's plan beckons us to look up. When we look up, we look straight to hope. Hope holds the answers to happiness and fulfillment. But even as we look up, we have a choice to remain inflexible or step into flexibility and go with the flow. When we resist or compromise, we cause this natural flow to stagnate. God has done his job and created the effortless flow; we need to do ours and go with it.

Sometimes it's tough to go with the flow. But being flexible involves recognizing a divine plan in our circumstances and learning how to detach from our own opinions, ideas, and outcomes. When we're flexible, we're open to different ways of seeing change. Flexibility allows our brain to think differently, and when that happens, it creates a new path of thought. The more we think in the new way, the deeper the groove is made along that thought path. The deeper the groove, the more the new thought is entrenched in our behavior. It takes a lot of bending for us to get unstuck and go with the flow, but in the end, the hard work pays off.

A fourteen-year age difference exists between my two children. This age gap created a challenge. Talk about gearing up for two separate generations—raising these kids was a real test. The structured discipline that worked with my daughter from the X generation was laughable to my son, the Y generation. Where Gen X was more inclined to respect authority, the Gen Y, or Millennial, child believed that everyone was equal in terms of respect, ambition, enmity. "Respect your elders" was as ridiculous to my younger child as a two-headed frog.

I came from the baby boomer generation, and while my peers and I may not have respected authority in its entirety, we did at least externally because we knew it was better to go with the flow, to be flexible. Imagine the degree of flexibility I needed in order to live under the same roof with my younger son, whose favorite toy was a computer and its gaming software. If my husband and I hoped to raise a decent Gen Y child, we had to let go of old ideals, becoming flexible enough to accept the notion of instant gratification while remaining character driven. Seeing life from our son's perspective helped us to find balance as we meshed the generational gap, and because of our son's propensity for fairness, he too was able to bend.

Bye-Bye, Comfort Zone

Most of us love our comfort zones. Why? Because they protect us. They create a sense of commonness in our lives—a place of familiarity, expected outcomes, security, and safety. We enjoy an anxiety-neutral environment in which we can glide through life without threat of risk and harness our security within predictable boundaries. We don't notice the path less traveled. Nothing new happens in our lives. We get stale and stuck, and we don't realize it. These are the trappings of a comfort zone.

Flexibility, on the other hand, allows us to grow bored with the old and enthusiastic for the new. The more we feed flexibility—a willingness to bend—the more it roots itself and takes its rightful place in our lives. We must always feed the behavior we want to keep. If we want to step outside our comfort zones and be open to something new, we need to feed flexibility.

The reality, however, is that we're on a narrow road when we step outside our comfort zone. Our anxiety level rises. We become stressed. But hold on! Don't give up! Give flexibility a try—go with the flow. The major benefit to this is that we learn new skills to help us deal with stress. It also opens our mind to accepting this new level of anxiety and how it can work in our favor. The further away from our comfort zone we move, the more flexible we become.

It's not necessary for us to take giant steps in our quest for a balanced life. The good news is that baby steps offer the best possible rate of success.

Conclusion

When the unexpected occurs, remain open to new possibilities. Bend with the winds of change. Practice your sway factor. Look for the new opportunities that can be discovered within change. With a little practice we can learn to be more flexible and adaptable. We can get into our sway and bend like the palm tree.

I've had challenges sneak into my life after I've purposed to be flexible, keep an open mind, step outside my comfort zone, go with the flow. Because of my commitment to new behaviors, I have been better prepared to handle these challenges and, most importantly, grow from them.

When I first made the decision to ignite my sway factor, I must admit, it was like swimming in circles in a bottomless swimming pool with no siding to hold on to for support, safety, and rescue. Instead of panicking, I did what I knew for sure to do, which was to go with the flow. Eventually my character grew stronger and my emotions were able to calm down enough to welcome the change.

Welcoming this intruder called change can help us face the fear that keeps us stuck in our resistance. We'll have the power to weaken fear's threat and gain confidence. Viktor Frankl, an Austrian neurologist and psychiatrist as well as a Holocaust survivor, offered a fitting quote that can help us bridge the gap to change: "When we are no longer able to change a situation, we are challenged to change ourselves."[1]

Flexibility says, "Go with the flow, and enjoy forward progress!"

Action Points

Why are the lessons gained from former life experiences important to your ability to remain flexible in any situation?

Psychologically speaking, experts say that fear is a learned behavior. Are you afraid of something through your own faulty thinking? Was fear taught to you by someone else? Either way, list your fear here, and write how you've dealt with it or need to deal with it.

What does flexibility look like in your life?

How can stubbornness stifle your progress to live a more flexible lifestyle?

What can you do to step out of your comfort zone and move toward a more flexible lifestyle?

10

Know Yourself, Find Your Purpose

Know thyself.

SOCRATES

We typically look into a mirror to get a good look at ourselves as we style our hair, apply makeup, check for anything odd that may be sticking between our teeth, or, if you're my age, check for wrinkles! After all, isn't that what mirrors are for? To ensure that we're put together? Presentable?

But when was the last time you looked in the mirror and smiled at who you saw? Or approved of yourself? Or were comfortable wrapped inside your own skin? Our brains are the collection center of everything we've heard about ourselves, either from others or our own thoughts. When we're judged by our looks, accomplishments, or status in society, our brains record the information and instantly search for that file whenever we need it. If the person we see in the mirror doesn't make us proud, our brains will find the appropriate file and begin to recite from it, saying, "Disappointment. Failure. Loser." This will be an obvious hindrance to reaching our goals to live balanced and purposeful lives.

The wonderful news about our brains is that the contents of each file can be changed. To learn how to change these files, let's discuss the importance of self-awareness and finding our own voices.

Self-Awareness Defined

No doubt you've used a two-sided mirror. One side provides a normal view, the other a magnified view. One morning as I started to apply makeup, I inadvertently used the magnified side, which nearly scared me to death. After overcoming my initial shock, I managed to study my face. Yikes! Wrinkles, large pores, blemishes, discoloration. The magnification made me keenly aware of my skin's condition and prompted me to take better care of it. After that brief epiphany, I tried to rest my pounding heart and return to the normal side of the mirror. But the wrinkles and large pores got me thinking about the fact that the magnifying mirror has benefits that are important to our well-being.

Like the magnifying mirror, self-awareness shines a spotlight on who we really are—our character and the unique qualities we offer to others. How we see ourselves determines how we fit into our environment—and at what depth we see our purpose in that environment. Knowing ourselves has the potential to make us alert to strengths within us that we should salute and weaknesses that we can grow into strengths.

Self-awareness is a journey toward self-discovery. It's about understanding different facets of ourselves—how we think, what we feel, how we react to a situation. Self-awareness causes a confidence to blossom within us that makes us comfortable living with ourselves.

Finding Your Voice Through Self-Awareness

Once we come to know ourselves and recognize our own significance, we're ready to find our voice—the truest expression of our character, beliefs, and passions. Self-awareness gives us the freedom to express our voice and communicate to others the lessons we've learned through past experiences so that they can be spared the pain we've encountered.

I'll never forget my first encounter with a wonderfully warm and helpful high-school biology teacher. His voice was filled with reason. He wasn't totally supportive of my end-of-year project to observe how carrot tops grew and behaved in different soils and environments, but he kept an open mind. His voice was collaborative. I learned from this man how to express my voice in a collaborative way when it came to issues I didn't entirely support. By the way, my experiment made the school-wide science fair.

We can get "voice lessons" not only from a collaborative teacher, but we can even learn from a difficult teacher who has lost her passion. She exists for a paycheck. She doesn't care if her class learns or not. Her responses to questions are indifferent. Her voice is saturated in anger. I learned from such a teacher the entrapment that unhappiness creates in a voice.

We are confronted with all kinds of voices expressing varying opinions and ideologies. While all of them can be quite convincing, we should remember that if we are to thrive, we need to find our own unique voice. Sure, we see people we admire and want to emulate, but they have their own purpose, and their voice reflects it. We should not rely on imitation as a shortcut to success. If we do, we will not live authentic lives, and the success we think we have found will be hollow and without a foundation. In order to fulfill the purpose God intended us to, each of us must *find our own voice.*

Actively Search for Your Voice

None of us will wake up one morning and identify our voices. Rather, finding our voices is an evolving process—a search. As children, we were exposed to different fields of knowledge and experience. Most of us didn't know what we wanted to become or what we were good at, but once we were exposed to education, we began the process of finding our voices. As adults, the process of finding our voices continued, and eventually it was groomed by our passion.

When I was a child, I loved to play teacher. I'd line up all my dolls and stuffed animals on the living-room sofa and use the coffee table as a desk. I'd play for hours, teaching my precious students how to read, write, and do math. But when I went to college, becoming a teacher never entered my mind. My major was in business, and later I found my niche in corporate America's management. But coincidentally, most jobs I had seemed to have a training component to them.

A few years later, I started a silk-flower business on the side as a creative outlet, and I taught floral arranging. My students told me, "You're so easy to follow!" I was surprised at my teaching skills, but these comments ignited my passion to teach. When I became an instructor for a professional association, the class made the same comments on their course evaluations. Again, I was surprised. Actually, I shouldn't have been surprised, especially when I thought back to my playtime as a child.

Nor should I have been surprised when I became passionate about writing articles for a business magazine. As a child, I'd had a strong inner wiggle and couldn't concentrate long enough to read two sentences. I had been a poor student, but I had excelled in creative thinking. I could tell a storyline without effort. Just give me a title, and off I'd go.

Most of us have had times when we wished we could follow our passion, but something always seemed to be in our way. In fact, you may say, "I have a good-paying job that's not my passion, but if I found my passion, it wouldn't even pay for a tank of gas." Hold on! Don't wait for your dream job to come around. Look for ways to find your voice where you are today. Where you are right now has a purpose. Find your voice in that purpose. You may love working with children, gardening, volunteering at an animal shelter, or traveling. Look for ways that you can develop your voice—today—because today holds opportunities! Your voice is equipped with the things you love. They were planted within you from the day you were born. God made sure you had the necessary equipping to live your dream. Don't let another day go to waste.

Follow your dream. Keep alert. One door will open, then another and another—you'll get there. Keep faithful. Keep focused. I have found my voice—in a way beyond anything imagined—since starting my company, Cornerstone Management Skills. The strength of my voice assures me that I'm where God intended me to be. In retrospect, though, my process to find my voice was a long search. It went all the way back to that little girl who taught her dolls and stuffed animals in her living room. It took me awhile to find my path, but when I did, I could see that it had been plotted out. I simply navigated my way from one open door to the next and eventually found my destiny.

Actively Listen to Others

People will come across our paths and with them a message and purpose that will help us navigate our travel. We can miss these people if we're distracted, but when we are alert and in tune with other people, we will be able to gather all kinds of information.

If we want to find our voices, we need to listen to the entire message of those who come into our lives. Not part of it—the whole thing. We should listen to people even if they share things we don't want to hear. We must keep an open mind. People come across our paths to help pilot our journeys, so we should listen to them actively. When we do so, we will learn to understand issues from the other party's point of view. This will help us discover our own voices through their creative solutions.

Self-Awareness Perspective: Life in Slow Motion

I recently attended a workshop led by Jeff Triplette, a well-known referee for the NFL. He told of his early days in the NFL—sprinting with athletes double his size who ran and weaved as fast as a snake set afire. How could he catch these guys in an error? Make the right call? Jeff asked his mentor these questions, and the advice was simple: "You gotta watch the game in slow motion."

I later e-mailed him and asked for a few tips to elaborate this point. This is what he wrote me back:

> You learn to "see things in slow motion" when you concentrate and focus your *entire* attention on a particular object or thing—like the movement of a baseball. (Can you see the seams as it travels ninety miles per hour or follow the pea in a shell game?)
>
> *Only* then does one begin to master the art of seeing things in slow motion. The brain and eyes are wonderful things—they can process so much information that when one focuses them on only one item, the power is overwhelming. Try it. It takes practice and relaxation—you'll know when you have it because you will see things you've never seen before.[1]

Try to watch yourself in slow motion by taking a breath and then a step backward. When we're totally immersed in self-awareness, we discover the truest expression of our character and passion. We're able to find the freedom to express our voices with confidence and boldness.

Develop Self-Awareness

It's a treat to observe a baby in self-discovery. She's captivated with the movements of her hand, and later she discovers her feet and those short, stubby toes. Her life is a wonder. Soon she's able to stand, discovering a world from a completely different vantage point than she has thus far. Unfortunately, this increase in self-awareness wanes as we grow up. Developing our own self-awareness is critical to making changes in our thoughts and interpretations of a situation. Changing our interpretations allows us to change our emotions and move beyond our pain to good solutions.

Self-awareness is the first step in creating the life we want and mastering our confidence and success. How we focus our attention, emotions, reactions, personality, and behavior determines our direction. Being self-aware is like following street signs as we drive down an unfamiliar road. We are able to see the path ahead of us and make necessary adjustments to stay focused and forward moving.

Ever find you're in a predicament and you don't know what to do? You're not able to see what controls your emotions, behavior, reactions. Because of this momentary shortsightedness, you lack the necessary insights to make changes in life that you had hoped to make. You know you'd be so much happier if you could make positive changes. The key is to know yourself—to be aware of who you are, what you do, why you do it.

As you make the journey to self-awareness, consider the following list of actions that can help facilitate self-awareness. I call these "yahoos," since we can enjoy the "yahoo" shout-outs when we've accomplished each of these action steps:

- Discover your true and unlimited potential.
- Concentrate on effective decision making.
- Create an environment that better suits your needs.
- Sustain positive change.
- Focus your energy and time on what you do best.

If you're able to carve out some quiet time for yourself, take some time to examine the five goals listed above, one at a time. This way you won't rush through a task that is better served with time and relaxation. Gaining a clear understanding of how each of these five goals can help you discover your voice is a good way to reexamine yourself while looking in the mirror.

When our sense of self is in order, we can be better aware of what God thinks of us. Have you ever thought of the depth of awareness God has for you? His unconditional love is documented throughout the Bible, most particularly in Psalm 139, which is entitled, "God's Perfect Knowledge of Humankind." King David, the author, is astounded that God himself has searched and knows him. God knew when he sat or stood or lay down. God even knew his thoughts from a far distance. He understood David's path and was acquainted with everything he did. Is it not then reasonable for us to ask ourselves, "If God is that keen on me, why am I not keen on myself? What is getting in my way of me accepting myself? What distracts my focus, my commitment, my determination?"

Difficult days can devour our resolve, dismantle our focus, and we wonder, "How did that happen?" Yesterday we were set ablaze with confidence, ambition, creative revelations; we went to sleep that person, but today we awoke a stranger. Now we toss and turn throughout the night, laboring over our big next day. Our self-worth fades away in the night. When this happens to me, I get out of bed and read Psalm 139. Its message is literally like comfort food for my anxious soul. I return to bed, feeling as if I can handle anything.

Psalm 139 reminds me that God knows my every thought. He is intimately concerned about me. He knows when I sit, stand, hop, or skip. He is consumed with thoughts of me. When the psalmist declares, "His thoughts of me exceed the grains of sand," I wonder, "Is David talking about only one beach?"

The next time you're at the beach, wiggle your toes deep in the sand; then think about all the other beaches all over the world. Now imagine how God's thoughts of you are beyond comprehension.

Discover What Matters Most

When it comes to self-awareness and discovery, Zig Ziglar tells us what matters most: "Put all excuses aside and remember this: YOU are capable."[2] What matters most after you've burnt dinner and there's nothing in the house to eat? What matters most when someone breaks into your locked car and steals your laptop? What matters most when the doctor gives you a bad report? All kinds of scenarios beg the question, but when we dig deep, we'll find that what matters most is simply that we are capable!

When we can answer this important question about what matters most, we will be better able to face the important issues in life. Little things don't matter that much: complaining doesn't matter; jealousy doesn't matter; anger is wasted energy. As with the old saying "We've got bigger fish to fry," after all the smoke blows away, what really matters is that *you* are capable of handling a tough situation or being brave enough to make an important change in your life.

We tend to forget our capabilities, and when we do, we allow unnecessary pressure on ourselves because we think it will motivate us to self-discovery. But to really know ourselves, we need to focus on the things our hearts find endearing—they're called matters of the heart, and they will not deceive us. Whatever our hearts find endearing are the things that will help us find our voices and give us grace to hold on to happy and fulfilled lives.

For example, when we hear a phrase or a word that resonates deep within our beings, we've found what really matters to us. When I hear the word "humble," I'm immediately drawn to it. Being humble, especially as I encourage others, means that I put my ego aside and become completely invested in the person I'm speaking with. Being humble means that I listen to someone and gather all the details of his or her story, and by doing this, I can provide that person relevant feedback. When I function in matters of my heart, I feel richer for the experience—it's a blessing. The things that matter to each of us will enable us to see all the blessings we possess in our lives and appreciate the strong foundations we already have.

One day I gave the endearing matters of my heart a good, hard look. At first my mind was a blank, but as I continued to focus, my mind became overloaded with happy thoughts. My family popped into my mind, then a fresh cup of coffee in the morning, then hearing the birds chirp as I stood on the balcony with my hot brew. My scope of thoughts expanded to friends and to all the simple yet wonderful things in life that are priceless. I focused on all those people and events that reminded me of how blessed I really was.

Self-Understanding Plus Self-Acceptance Equals Forgiveness

Experts encourage us to forgive offenders, not for the offenders' sakes but our own. But to actually forgive someone who has hurt us deeply is easier said than done. Still, we can become brave enough to forgive someone by first trying to understand that person. This means taking a step back, putting our pain aside while we look objectively at the situation, and trying to understand why the person did what he did. In other words, we need to put ourselves in that person's shoes. Once we're able to figure the individual out, the next step automatically follows: accepting their behavior—not to condone it but to accept it for what it is.

Sometimes, however, the hardest person to forgive is ourselves. But the same is true of forgiving ourselves as it is of forgiving others: when we see the real us in the mirror, it can become an adventure in accepting ourselves—and thus understanding our true potential.

If you are bogged down with the cares of life, you may be thinking that your joy is unrecoverable—too many bad experiences have robbed you of your good attitude. Perhaps someone hurt you, and when the relationship was severed, a piece of yourself was left with that person. How can you forgive? How can you let go? As difficult as it might be, look at the hurt as a gift. It was meant to groom you, not harm you. Once you recognize that the person who hurt you was given as a special gift, you can come to the place at which you're able to forgive.

For years I was held prisoner by a hurt, but then I realized I had actually grown from the experience. The new softness of my heart made me thankful for the painful experience, and I was able to find myself by forgiving that person. Forgiveness can heal us from hurt and disappointment and free us from standing weakly in our pain. When we forgive others and ourselves, we grow in character and find our truest selves.

Forgiveness is not only liberating; it also removes blinders from our eyes. It helps us see ourselves more clearly, and many times after we forgive, we decide that we like what we see. Because of the peace we feel, we are able to truly like ourselves, and when we like ourselves, we are keen to become self-aware and self-accepting.

Be Kind to Yourself

Kindness is an attribute that opens a window into our sense of self. Want to enlarge your capacity to be kind to others? First be kind to yourself. Cut the same amount of slack for yourself that you do for others. Don't rob yourself of the gift of kindness. When we can grow in the warmth of self-kindness, we are better prepared to accept others, who are then likely to respond to us with encouragement and support. When we accept others and the support they bring, we will find that our own self-esteem is improved.

I used to have a habit of calling myself a dummy whenever I made a misstep. I'd stub my toe and say, "Dummy." I'd bounce a check—"Dummy." I'd forget to put leftovers in the refrigerator on a hot evening and would have to toss it in the trash the next morning: "Big dummy. Now you have to cook!"

One day I heard a preacher warn against people criticizing themselves. He said that when we speak harshly of ourselves, what we're really saying is that God makes junk. Honestly, I nearly fell out of the church pew, because there is *no way* that God could make any junk. As I gave that sermon some thought, I realized that the preacher was right! When I put myself down, I *was* saying that God makes junk! (Sorry, Lord!) When I cleaned up those demeaning thoughts against myself, I noticed that my critical point of view of others changed as well.

Keep Getting Better

Other people's opinions of us don't have to become our reality. Take a risk. Embark upon a path you'd normally shy away from. Follow your heart. Create a new normal for yourself. Only then can the right people enter your life—those who have the capability to promote you, mentor you, hold the pieces of your dream together until those pieces form into promise. Never ever give up on yourself.

Conclusion

As a child, I was overweight. Kids at school called me "Carol, Carol, big fat barrel." Not only was my body big, my hair was even bigger, since I had been forced to suffer through the bad perms my mom gave me. The worst part was that my mom bragged about how cute I was. Funny, her friends never said a word in reply. In addition to my hair troubles, I was a slow learner at school; studies didn't come easily to me back then. In short, I didn't like myself—until one day I was introduced to myself.

Over the years I've learned that the more I know me, the happier I am with me. Sure, there are a few things that could use some polish—well, okay, a lot of things—but those will come in due time—when I'm ready. God will see to that. Why? Because his greatest desire is for each of us to aspire to our highest calling.

Are you in?

Action Points

Why is self-acceptance the key to unlocking your ability to be flexible in tough situations?

How does finding your own voice pave the way to improved self-awareness?

Does your mind tend to wander when you're listening to another person? Listening to a person's entire story is key to finding your own voice. Think of a conversation in which you didn't listen to the whole story. How did it compromise the fullness of your voice?

Take a moment to read Psalm 139. How does it make you feel? What is your takeaway?

Why is self-understanding important to self-acceptance?

How does kindness play a major role in self-awareness?

11

Being the Best *You* Possible

If you will call your troubles experiences, and remember that every experience develops some latent force within you, you will grow vigorous and happy, however adverse your circumstances may seem to be.

JAMES RUSSELL MILLER

Boxes come in every shape and size, and each has a special purpose, whether it's a tool box, a ring box, a tackle box, a jewelry box, a storage box, a deck box, a clothes box, a shoe box, or a mail box. I wouldn't use my husband's smelly fishing-tackle box for a pair of my shoes. And he wouldn't use my shoe box for his slimy hooks and lures. A shoe box is intended to hold one pair of shoes, while a tackle box is equipped with all kinds of separate compartments and shelves to hold a myriad of fishing accessories to make that big catch.

Each of us is made to walk a distinct journey in life, and therefore each of us is made with our own special type of box. Our boxes, or our minds, hold a collection of all our personal life experiences. This collection consists of not only the good lessons we've learned but also the negative outcomes of some of our experiences, like the negative thoughts or words we've held about a failure or the way we should have known better about handling a situation or making a decision. Yes, every deed, every thought—everything we've experienced—is in our boxes. Some of the items in my box may be similar to yours, but they are not identical, and that's what makes each and every one of us unique.

Embracing our uniqueness produces joy and fulfillment and helps us live out the distinct purpose for which each of us was made.

You're Unique!

Have you taken the time to consider how unique you are? How special? How valued? When was the last time you recognized the unique value you add to your home, office, church, community? It's like our fingerprints, which are distinctive to each of us personally; scientists say there isn't a duplicate fingerprint in any two people in the whole wide world. You've got to admit, that's pretty amazing. That makes each of us one of a kind.

In chapter 10 we discussed the importance of acknowledging our individuality from the point of view of Psalm 139 in the Bible. Let's consider other verses in this psalm in terms of God's opinion of us and how we can let loose unwanted character traits from our box: "You created my inmost being; you knit me together in my mother's womb. I praise you because I am fearfully and wonderfully made; your works are wonderful" (Psalm 139:13–14).

Did you catch the sense of awe in what the psalmist David said about his own unique qualities? Think about him checking out his hands, legs, feet, fingers, ears and realizing that God had known him while he was still in his mother's womb. History shows that

David was the lad who killed the giant Goliath and later became the most magnificent king of Israel. Most importantly, however, he was favored by God. In fact, his name means "beloved." Even though history doesn't say much about you and me, these verses in Psalm 139 call out your name, my name, everybody's name. You and I, like David, were fearfully and wonderfully made.

You may be thinking, *What about a child born with spina bifida? Or someone who lost her sight after a freak accident? What's wonderful about these conditions?* Yet even these things have a very special purpose.

I had the honor of knowing Ken, a man who changed my life. He suffered from cerebral palsy. Nearly every afternoon, as I walked home from elementary school as a child, he wheeled himself along the sidewalk. With his hand bent at the wrist and fingers spread out like crooked bird feathers, Ken tried to talk to me as the sunlight glistened in the drool that slipped down his chin. Frightened, I dashed across the street to avoid him.

Years later as a young adult, I had the privilege of meeting him again at church. His speech was still thick and awkward, but eventually I was able to understand him better and laugh at his teasing.

One day when our church group visited inmates at a local jail, I sat on the grass next to Ken's wheelchair as we visited with the detainees. Suddenly Ken gestured wildly and mumbled for a drink of water. I nearly froze. I looked around for someone to help him. But everyone else was busy talking with detainees. All 100 billion nerve cells in my body began to freak out. I looked around again for someone to help Ken and finally realized that this one was on me. I finally dug my hand into a pocket in his backpack to retrieve a large mug of water with an oversized straw. I carefully slipped the straw between his lips, and he drank that mug dry and smiled. I found a cloth napkin in his backpack and dabbed drool from his chin, remembering how he had frightened me as a child.

A few minutes later I froze again when he asked me to feed him.

"Sure, Ken." I forced a laughed through the tenseness in my throat. "Sure, if you'll let me have every other bite," I teased, trying to hide my own awkwardness. His mother had cut a sandwich into small bites. I took each piece and placed it in his mouth, his drool sticking to my fingertips. Just before each bite, he thanked me, again and again. With every inch of his body shifting erratically, he struggled to mutter words of thanks. When he finished, I sat back down at his side—changed.

Ken's humble gratitude and crooked smile bore through my own tongue-tied heart. All the frozenness had left me. In that moment I came to realize that Ken was fearfully and wonderfully made.

What Were You Created For?

What comes to your mind when you think about God's wonderful plan in his creation of you? For me, I can't believe that the Creator took time out of his busy schedule to form me. He protected me while I was in my mother's womb and made sure I was created the way he intended. My heart brims with gratitude that the God of the universe thought me special enough to make me wonderfully. Now I'm motivated! I understand that I have been equipped with a very special box. My priority is to keep my box uncluttered and store only those items in it that help me stay focused on my particular destiny: reaching out to others and helping them live joyously.

Some of us may not have a clue as to what our destiny is. We're stuck in a job we don't want, yet we have no idea what we *do* want to do. But sometimes we *need* to be wedged in a place of immobility, because it enables us to think outside our situation and search our box for a remedy.

At times it's hard to let go of bad attitudes about ourselves, because some of us have told ourselves for a long time that we're a disappointment. A failure. A loser. Isn't it time we clean out our boxes and lighten our load as we continue our journey toward a joyful, abundant life?

This journey has one criterion: no pondering of negative thoughts. Every time a negative thought speeds across your mind, *stop!* Replace it with an antonym. If your mind says, "You're lazy," find words with an opposite meaning: "I'm productive. I get things done!" Here's another tip: if your mind says that you've been lazy, and you have been, then acknowledge that as truth and vow to change.

Once new, positive information is stored in your box, guard that information. If you don't, the negative words you're used to hearing will try to crawl back in. Whenever you get sidetracked and your mind returns to old thoughts of yourself, remember that God had a special purpose in mind when he created you, and because of your purpose, he has assigned a special box to you. That purpose formed your personality, talents, likes, dislikes, and mannerisms. God took special care to tailor you according to his grand plan. If anyone were to search this world for someone exactly like you, none would be found.

No Fair Comparing Yourself to Others

Let's face it—we tend to compare our boxes with others'. It's really unfair to compare ourselves, though, because each of us is incomparable. It's like comparing the value and purpose of a Mercedes to that of a Porsche. Each is a high-end vehicle, but one is a luxury vehicle, the other for sport. At the end of the day, how effective is it to compare the incomparable?

If we give into comparing ourselves, we find that there is no end to this type of behavior. Comparison is a trap, because we always seem to want what we don't have. I envy gals with naturally curly hair. And of course, women with curly hair hate it, wishing they had straight hair. The list of comparisons distracts us from who we are. If we insist on measuring up to others, we'll never fulfill our true potential. We'll never fill our own boxes with the right stuff. The way to step up our game is not to see who had the highest work productivity this month, who won the award for mom of the year, who's getting bonuses and promotions. Really, isn't that a waste of good energy?

Why not put good energy to work on your own behalf? Run your own race with your own box. Every time. No matter what.

Someone Else May Need What You Have in Your Box

We've all gone through some tough experiences and wondered, "Why me?" But in the aftermath of our challenges, we often realize that a difficult experience we have weathered has become a gift for someone else. The lessons we learned in it become our truths, and we're able to help others from those truths and hopefully save them from heartbreak and frustration.

The guidance we've received from life experiences should go into our box. Fill your box with what you know is truth for you—what you know for sure. If you don't, when someone needs something from your box—those jewels from your life that will help make that person's life better—you'll regret having to rummage through the junk to find the good things they need.

When someone needs something from your box, be generous. Give yourself away. Give away those precious gems you've collected while learning lessons from life events. What you've learned is paramount for building character, growing confidence, and strengthening backbone. By unequivocally giving yourself away, you help others by equipping them with ideas from your character, confidence, and courage.

Several years after my husband's and my family life had settled and our son was no longer running away from home, a friend called, asking me to help a friend of hers. She explained that her friend's son kept running away. She and her husband had tried everything to keep him home, to get him help, but nothing seemed to work. I spoke with her friend, listening to her heartache and disappointment and how her marriage was now on a slippery slope. I knew exactly what she felt. I had lived it for years. But now I was able to go into my box and pull out words of encouragement and tips on how to cope, how to stay strong, how to rely on God. I was able to give myself away to her and let her know that she wasn't alone.

What precious gems can you pull from your box to help someone else? Never hesitate to be that miracle in giving yourself away, even if you have to relive your pain. In the end it will be worth it, because we can never out-give ourselves. When we give ourselves away, we always get a better, richer part of ourselves back.

Take an Inventory

My aunt uses a spare bedroom as a dumping place for things she doesn't know what to do with. The room is such a mess that she keeps the door closed. The only time she opens it is to toss something else inside. She calls that room the McGee Room (from the 1950s radio sitcom *Fibber McGee & Molly*, which comically featured the couple's bulging messy closet).

I had heard about my aunt's room, so one day when I visited her, I peeked into it. My eyes popped wide as I scanned the mountain of clutter on the bed, the chest of drawers, the floor, and what was once the nightstand. She passed by and said, "I've got to clean that mess." I asked if she knew what was in there. She laughed and gave a list of things that she really should throw out. But of course, some things she still needed and wouldn't throw away. I glanced through the room again, and sure enough, I saw a few things she had mentioned: an old robe; a pair of faded bedroom slippers; a small, fake, haphazardly decorated Christmas tree that had fallen over.

Just as it had become easier over time for my aunt to toss unwanted things in the McGee Room, so too it becomes easy for us to throw junk into our boxes. Before we realize it, we've got a mess on our hands. Think of a closet in your home that needs to be cleaned out. Like my aunt did, you too could probably make a list of all the things that need to be tossed, of the things you haven't used for a while. You know what they are—those clothes that no longer fit but that you hang on to because you *might* lose weight! Our boxes may suffer the same predicament.

You're probably able to make a list of all the junk you've been carrying in your box: negative thoughts, a judgmental attitude, sorrow over regrets. If you don't make a conscious list of what to throw away, you'll procrastinate in cleaning out your box. When it comes to maintaining a healthy box, less is more. In other words, we need fewer bad attitudes and negative thoughts. When we minimize these, we will have more room to fill our boxes with our personal-quality DNA.

Spring Cleaning

As a teenager, I dreaded helping my mom spring clean our house. Every year we moved furniture, dusted, scrubbed, vacuumed, polished. What a job. Dusting my mom's vast collection of Asian knickknacks was like trying to figure out where to start sorting through a garage that hadn't been cleaned for at least a century. What made matters worse for me was when I didn't clean every micro inch of her collectibles. She'd spot that minuscule dot of dust from across the room, and I'd have to start dusting those ugly things all over again. Maddening! After finally finishing the dusting, I dragged my exhausted body to my next assignment—cleaning out closets and getting rid of things we hadn't used in the past year. Mom and I were like two bulldozers carrying armfuls of junk outside for a Goodwill pickup.

Days later when we were (finally) finished, the house smelled fresh, and everything sparkled (even those ugly figurines). I'd be the first to say that spring cleaning is a drag, but the hard work always pays off. In the same way, we should clean out our boxes and keep only those things that build character and allow room for new experiences. This way we won't haul old baggage into new opportunities.

Once our boxes have been cleaned out, it's important that we don't throw old things back in. Life events are gifts to stretch us, make us grow, mature us, improve our character, and, many times, increase the size of our hearts to make room for more compassion, empathy, understanding, and caring for others. Those are the kinds of things we should keep in our boxes.

When you clean out your box, throw out the negative things people have said about you, and recount your own virtues—who you really are. Find anything in your box that doesn't promote you, edify you, or confirm a positive attitude about you, and get rid of them.

Why is it important to periodically inventory our boxes and clean them up? There are many reasons, but the primary one is that we eventually become what we carry in our boxes. When calamity inches into our lives, we subconsciously go to our boxes to find the tools we need to cope. If we have junk in our boxes, that's what we'll use, and it will weaken our ability to cope and deal effectively with our issues.

Several years after our son seemed to settle down after his continual running away, I found myself reliving those heartbreaking episodes as though they had just happened. My open wounds of raw disappointment, rejection, and abandonment kept my heart injured and wronged. When family or friends inquired about how my son was now doing, my body tensed, my heart pounded, my thoughts scattered. Words clogged in my throat. Anger flared with memories of hurt and regret.

One day I asked myself why I was still so deeply hurt from an experience that had happened years ago. I took some time to be still, and the answer came. I was holding on to things in my box. Yes, these things made me unhappy, but that unhappiness had become a delusional place of comfort. It was hard, but I had to admit that there was junk in my box. I dug into it and hauled out thoughts that were no longer true, that were holding me back.

I found that the biggest junk piece in my box, however, although it made me utterly unhappy, was tough to let go. It was unforgiveness. I held on to anger because I hadn't forgiven our son for making my life miserable or nearly destroying my marriage or causing me nights of sleeplessness or making me wonder if he was dead, alive, safe, if another mom was feeding him, if he would ever come home. As I pondered the anger and unforgiveness in my box, old wounds of abandonment from my childhood, of being left with people I hadn't known while my mother traveled, were aggravated. I had always felt as if I wasn't good enough and that this was why I had been left behind. When my son had run away, I had likewise thought that maybe I wasn't good enough to be his mom. He must have hated me to leave. But why? I had tried my best to be a good mom, a fun mom. Why hadn't he accepted me? I rocked back and forth, trying to find a place that didn't hurt. Then a word was whispered in my mind: "Forgiveness."

But maddening as my unhappiness was, I didn't want to forgive my son. I was angry. I wanted to keep him in my trap. But the trap was for me. I was trapping myself with unforgiveness. One night I couldn't live with the misery anymore, and I was finally able to cry out, "Son, I forgive you." Suddenly it felt as though the elephant I had carried around for so many months just up and left. After forgiving my son, I was able to forgive myself for what I had perceived as my own troubles and for forgetting that my son had been struggling with his own sense of self-worth and value.

Do you see what happened here? When I found the source of my heartache, confessing it cleared the way to fully understanding my situation. I then had to offer forgiveness, and doing that cleared the way to understanding that my son's angst hadn't been against me personally. He had been trying to find his own way during an extremely difficult time in his early teenage years. Forgiveness helped me step back and clearly see that I could throw away the measuring stick that I had used to evaluate myself unrealistically. Still, old thoughts are hard to break, and from time to time, negativity crawled back into my box, causing me to say, "I'm not good enough." But I tossed it out again and again until my box held only those experiences that challenged and grew my character.

Conclusion

What's in your box? Take an inventory of the attitudes that may be holding you back—thoughts of inadequacy or guilt. Get rid of them. God never intended you to hold on to the pollution in your life. You are highly valued, and therefore you deserve to live in total freedom. Once you're at that place of freedom, check the contents of your box, and keep only those unique qualities that make up the best of who you are.

Action Points

Life calls upon people to help others—to share life experiences, support others, encourage people. What things have you collected in your box that might help others?

Spring cleaning is helpful and sometimes needful to help you get rid of clutter. What things in your box should be tossed out?

Is unforgiveness filling up your box? Don't you think it's time to get rid of it? Share your story in a few words, and identify who needs your forgiveness and why.

How often should you do a good spring cleaning in your box? Make a commitment to do a thorough cleaning on a regular basis.

Make a list of all the character traits you want to keep in your box.

_____
_____
_____

Now make a list of all the junk you want to clean out.

_____
_____
_____

Do you agree with the psalmist, David, about being fearfully and wonderfully made? Jot down your thoughts.

_____
_____
_____

12

Keeping a Healthy Frame of Mind

*The pleasantest things in the world are pleasant thoughts;
and the great art of life is to have as many of them as possible.*

MONTAIGNE

During our family's first camping trip, my husband insisted upon packing a first aid kit for any injuries we might encounter while out in the wild. And really, it was the wild for me. I had grown up in the city, where first aid kits were mounted on school walls, in the nurse's room, in the gym, or in the employee lounge. Toting one on a vacation was the furthest thing from my mind. But it came in handy when one of our sons tripped on a hiking trip. My husband was able to fly into action and bandage our son's hands, elbows, and knees. Poor little guy! I soon learned that for a bee sting, a cut, or a sliver in a child's finger, a well-stocked first aid kit could be extremely helpful.

First aid kits are designed to care for injuries sustained from specific activities like hiking, camping, or boating. But we can create one for a definite need, even, yes, you guessed it, a first aid kit for our minds. So let's put one together—one that has everything necessary to help us keep a positive focus on our goals and aspirations and maintain a you-phoria state of mind.

First Aid Instruction Booklet

A first aid manual is critical for helping ease an injured person's pain and discomfort. Without its instructions and tips, a person may waste time and resources in a challenging situation. A manual for our minds can help us too, by guiding us to see the best in ourselves and maintain a healthy mind-set. This is vital to living a balanced life.

If I were to create a manual for keeping a healthy frame of mind, I would include several guidelines.

Preparation: feed your mind. We all fall into the same trap—we go into panic mode if we run into conflict or change and find that we have no resources to deal with it. It's important that we stock up in advance for an emergency so that when a tough situation develops, we are ready to take care of it.

When it comes to preparing ahead of time for my mental health, I follow a daily routine of reading a devotional book. The daily entry gives me a healthy dose of positive thinking that equips me for the day. Of course, at times I've been too busy for devotions and have come up a bit dry when a conflict or life surprise happens. This has reminded me that being prepared is invaluable to my success.

Warning: guard your mind. The information-gathering capacity of our brains is, well, mindboggling. Imagine how much information bombards us all day long. We read, hear, and see things from all kinds of influences that are recorded in our brains. Some of it is healthy and progressive, but some of it can bog us down, discourage us, and disillusion us. We need to guard our minds against these negative influences.

How we label ourselves is also critical to the overall welfare of our minds. Names can build or destroy the foundation of our attitudes. We stub our toe and shout, "Klutz!" We can't seem to stay in a relationship, and we angrily say, "Unlovable!" These names train us to give up, and when we do, we whisper, "Loser." Sadly, we learn to live up to these negative names. For everyday woes that try to rob us of our happiness, work on this tip: think on things that are true, things worthy of respect, whatever brings you awe—use positive labels to encourage, strengthen, and anchor yourself. When we do this, we guard our minds.

Step-by-step instructions: maintain a healthy mind. One negative thought can wipe out a host of positive ones. The first instruction for maintaining a healthy mind is obvious: stop negative thinking. Replace it with a thought that is the direct opposite of the negative thought.

The other day I made homemade granola for the second time in a month. Confident that I could remember the recipe, I didn't take time to read it, and I set the oven at 325 degrees instead of 225. Halfway into the baking time, I smelled something burning. I dashed into the kitchen, grabbed a potholder, swung open the oven door, and saw a plume of smoke bellow out. *Oh, the poor granola*, I thought. I set the tray on the stove and waved my mittened hand over the charred mess to chase away the smoke. What had gone wrong?

When I discovered that I had guessed the temperature incorrectly, a trove of nasty words spit out of my mouth: "Big dummy! What's wrong with you? Can't you remember a simple recipe? You're useless." Name calling ruined my day, and everything I did that day had to be done over. Why? Stinkin' thinkin' had been programmed into my mind.

So I did what I'm asking you to do—*stop the stinkin' thinkin', and tell yourself the direct opposite!* Here was my opposite: "Don't take the recipe for granted; read every detail. The next time you bake, take a moment to double check the temperature and time. A stitch in time saves nine." This line of positive thinking cut the sense of failure out of my mental bandwidth. Nothing will keep us down like calling ourselves things such as "failure." Instead, *stop*! Call yourself by a positive name.

Emergency Contact List

In an emergency, the last thing we need is to waste time hunting down phone numbers. I learned this lesson the hard way—ugh! While packing for a recent vacation, my husband checked his supply of vitamins, supplements, and prescriptions. We packed our fifth wheel with a large basket of all his vital stuff and headed to our favorite desert camping retreat, Cattail Cove in Lake Havasu, Arizona.

One morning my husband joined me outside where I was enjoying a cup of brew and the early desert sunrise. "Um," I heard my husband say shyly, "I need more tablets."

"How can that be? You checked them before we left!" I said with furrowed brow.

"Um, I must have miscounted."

We wasted three hours calling our pharmacy at home, searching for his doctor's phone number, securing his doctor's approval to fill the prescription in a different state, and calling 411 to find a pharmacy. Our day could have gone so much better if we'd had an emergency contact list.

Our minds need a list for handling emergencies as well. It can be a handy notepad of positive thoughts, affirmations, and reflective and stimulating phrases. I have a list recorded in an app called "Google Keep" in my iPhone. Here's a sample of my "plus thoughts":

- This too will pass.
- Let go and let God.

- What doesn't kill you makes you strong.
- Keep looking up!
- Be thankful!
- The best things in life are yours for the choosing.
- Have you laughed today?

This handy resource helps me change any stinkin' thinkin' when it first starts. If I allow a negative outlook within an inch of my thoughts, that crazy attitude will try to take a mile—and then my entire day is ruined. Since most of us are tethered to our cell phones, using it to refer to positive thoughts at a glance is convenient and helpful. Truthfully, some days we need all the help we can get!

Antiseptic Wipes

Every so often it's a good idea to use an imaginary cleaning cloth to dust the stinkin' thinkin' from our minds, because if we don't, negativity will pollute our thoughts. Many of us know that negative thoughts come more easily than positive ones, but we can't afford the luxury of a negative thought.

When a demeaning thought creeps up, *stop*! Trash the thoughts that contaminate your mind, and make positive thinking a habit. After all, you're special enough to deserve exceptional thoughts of who you are. Have a searching conversation with your soul—the birthplace of positive thoughts, and don't hesitate to find a strong antiseptic wipe of good thoughts to freshen up your attitude.

Gauze Pads and Adhesive Tape

What use is a gauze pad if you don't have anything to secure it to a wound? Some pairings logically go together—pen and paper, car and car keys, flashlight and batteries—but separately the items are useless. Our minds also need combos to keep us in a forward-moving motion. Think about a plan without action, an affirmation without conviction, facts without honesty, dreams without commitment.

We can have plans, affirmations, facts, and dreams, but to be successful we need to pair them with action, conviction, honesty, and commitment. Otherwise, meeting our goals will be as effective as having sterile gauze pads without adhesive tape.

Tweezers

Tweezers are useful for pulling out debris embedded in our skin or under our fingernails. Tweezers that I call "attitude" can remove the thorn of strife or whatever irritates our sense of well-being. Attitude tweezers stem from our personal inner growth, and this emerges when we get rid of the stuff that bogs us down.

The lessons we've learned in life eventually become our tweezers as well. That's why it's important that we learn from life experiences and never let these gems go to waste. The more we learn through life experiences, the more helpful our tweezers become for keeping negative thoughts from robbing us of our happiness.

Tweezers can also be that small inner voice warning us against the tempting wrong road. They might even nudge at our pocketbook during a fantastic sale at Nordstrom's, Bass Pro Shop, or Macy's to help us meet our financial goals!

Bandages

The Red Cross recommends including twenty-five bandages in a standard first aid kit for a family of four. Why so many? Perhaps for frequent changes to keep a wound fresh for healing. The need to change a bandage frequently mirrors our need to challenge our minds that often suffer from boredom: doing the same thing, hearing the same music, driving the same roads. Stimulate your mind! Meet new people. Read books in a different genre. Eat something new.

Voltaire, the famous French Enlightenment writer, said, "If we do not find anything very pleasant, at least we shall find something new."[1] When we don't discover anything new in our lives, we can easily fall into a rut.

You may say, "I like my ruts. They're safe."

Think about this simple truth: when comfort and sameness cause our imaginations to go flat, our desires for new things are flatlined. Why? Because we become bored and listless; nothing in life is exciting. If we stay within the four walls of our safe habits, predictability becomes unhealthy. That's when we've left the bandages on too long. Get some fresh air on those old practices.

Be challenged today to put on some brand-new bandages. Take a risk and use Hello Kitty or Ninja Turtle bandages. Do something you haven't done. Go somewhere you haven't been. Eat something exotic. Step outside your norm, and begin to live, explore, shake your tail feathers and find *yourself*—that special you that's been lost in the dullness of life.

Cold Packs

One day my husband gathered his clubs for a round of golf. As he turned toward the front door, I noticed an icepack tucked under his belt at the back of his trousers. I told him it didn't make sense to start a game if he had an aching back. Why not stay home and rest up? He smiled, and out the door he went. Later in the afternoon when he returned, I asked about his golf game. He smiled, held up the thawed icepack, and said, "This icepack saved the day."

In the same way an icepack reduces swelling in aching muscles, so too we can use an icepack for our minds to cool down stress. When was the last time you took a little time for yourself? It could be as simple as taking a short walk during a work break, stopping off at the mall on a Friday after work for an hour (or two) of window shopping, putting your feet up and letting the kids know that you need a few minutes of "me" time before starting dinner. Sit back. Feel the coolness of relaxing your mind.

Flashlight and Batteries

You left something outside and are looking for it at night. The street lights don't cast enough light. What you need is a flashlight. That is, one with charged batteries. It can be quite frustrating to need a flashlight only to discover that the batteries are dead.

A flashlight for our minds can help illuminate our choices while navigating life experiences. The flashlight could be a positive thought or a wise word that enlightens the path ahead of us. In my search for wisdom, a good flashlight has been the Bible. Over the years it has been my rock, and I've discovered that God has addressed and provided a solution for every situation in life. It's all right there in the Bible. Whenever I'm stumped, I search the Bible and find a solution, guidance, wisdom—whatever you want to call it—and a light is cast on my situation. Whenever I rely upon myself, however—when I think I don't need a flashlight—my life gets all tangled up.

When the unexpected happens along our journeys, most of us immediately feel a sense of lost control. If we only knew which road to take, most of us would say that a flashlight (with fully charged batteries, of course) would help shed light on the path ahead.

Conclusion

Are you ready to stock up your own personalized first aid kit? Once you've created your kit, be sure to check it regularly. Since the ultimate outcome of having such a kit is to prepare us for emergencies and, ultimately, help us grow from the difficult life experiences we encounter, we need to make sure that the items inside it don't expire or become useless. Look for ways to upgrade your thoughts and gain wisdom so that you can manage any situation.

Action Points

Your life experiences have equipped you with a personalized first aid kit for your mind. This chapter discussed including certain items in your first aid manual:

- Preparation (feeding your mind)
- Warnings (guarding your mind)
- Step-by-step instructions (keeping a healthy mind)

Would you add anything to this list? If so, what would it be?

List all the important people and sayings you would include in an emergency contact list.

It is easy to sulk in stinkin' thinkin' from time to time. What steps would you take to change your thought patterns?

What benefit would sterile pads be without adhesive tape? Without tape, it would be a struggle to keep the pad affixed to a wound. This chapter listed things that separate from each other would be virtually useless: a plan without action, affirmation without conviction, facts without honesty, dreams without commitment. Which of these combinations apply to your life?

Tweezers can remove a thorn of strife or whatever irritates your sense of well-being. Inner growth happens when you get rid of the stuff that bogs you down. What types of irritants would you use "tweezers" to help you to get rid of?

Experts recommend having a healthy supply of bandages to keep wounds clean and promote healing. What kinds of "bandages" would you need in your life to heal your hurts?

Icepacks provide ready relief for aching muscles. This concept can remind you to cool down your stress. What can you do to reduce stress in your life?

_____
_____
_____
_____
_____

It's helpful to have a "flashlight" while traveling through life's experiences. This could be a positive thought or a wise word that will illuminate the path ahead of you. What personal affirmations could help to light up your life's path and make your travel better?

_____
_____
_____
_____

13

Avoiding the Occupational Hazard of Burnout

My candle burns at both ends; it will not last the night.

EDNA ST. VINCENT MILLAY

We've all been here a time or two—okay, on several occasions—going like ninety, working long hours, burning the candle at both ends, setting the world on fire in our efforts to live purposeful, fulfilled lives. But such accelerated behavior comes with a price. When constant stress has us feeling disillusioned, helpless, and completely worn out, we may be suffering from burnout. When we're burned out, problems seem insurmountable, everything looks big and bleak, and it's difficult to muster up the energy to care about our situation, let alone do something about it.

Unfortunately, burnout sneaks up on us, and we don't realize that we're toast until smoke gets in our eyes. Burnout is a condition caused by imbalance: charging forward in the fast lane, being a workaholic or a perfectionist, and stretching ourselves too far, all of which cause us to lose our sense of center.

Burnout and Its Companion, Stress

Burnout is suffocating, don't you agree? Its negative effects spill over into every area of life: work, home, social, spiritual. If you are utterly stressed, have you wondered why? You may actually be burned out, not stressed out. Burnout may be the *result* of unrelenting stress, but it isn't the same as too much stress.

Stress involves feelings of *too much*: too many pressures that demand too much of us, both physically and mentally. Stressed people can still imagine, and they will feel better when they get their lives under some kind of manageable control.

Burnout, or feeling used up, is simply about *not enough*. There's not enough energy, imagination, or strength to put forth the normal effort of setting one foot in front of the other. People experiencing total exhaustion often don't see any hope of positive change in their situation. If excessive stress is like drowning in responsibilities, burnout is being all dried up. Here's an important difference to gauge between being stressed and burned out: we're usually aware of it when we are under a lot of stress, but we don't always notice burnout when it happens.

Let's take a closer look at the factors that cause this gnarly beast.

Causes of Burnout

Since burnout creeps up and catches us unaware, let's consider its causes. In most cases it stems from our jobs, including the job of stay-at-home mom—when we're at risk of exhaustion, or burnout, if we feel overworked and undervalued.

But feelings of being used up are not caused solely by stressful work or too many responsibilities. Other factors include lifestyle and certain personality traits. What we do in our downtime and how we look at the world can play just as big a role in causing burnout as overwork.

Perhaps one of the biggest culprits of burnout is having little or no control over an event.

Poor diet and lack of rest also play a major role. I'm learning to drink several glasses of water a day, but sometimes when I'm going like ninety, water is the last thing on my mind. But I've also learned what it feels like to be dehydrated—not fun. So I keep a large glass of water at my work station and another in my car, and these are goods reminder to drink up. Cheers!

Other factors lurk in the background of our drivenness and ambition. Are you a perfectionist? A pessimist? A control freak? A high achiever? A type A personality? Then you're a sure target for burnout. Do you suffer from an illness that just hangs on? Anxiety? Depression? Are you utterly overwhelmed? Does everything under the sun seem to require too much effort? Do you feel trapped and hopeless?

We've all felt a few of these symptoms. But when we're in the midst of them, how do we stop our world long enough to take a breath? Find a detour? Get back to center and live life joyously? Let's look at several tips.

Pace Yourself

Speeding trains slow down at intersections. Even God rested after he created the world. So we, all the more, need to slow down, rest, and pace ourselves. Our bodies weren't designed to go full speed all the time. There are several effective ways in which we can pace ourselves.

Mini breaks. Consider taking mini breaks throughout the day. For example, try sitting outside and enjoying nature. Take a short walk, and let the sun warm up and loosen the tension throughout your body. You'll be surprised at how a short walk has the capability of releasing cooped-up tension. If you can't get away, close your eyes at your desk, in the kitchen, in the car while you're waiting for your child to get out of school, or wherever you are and just chill out for at least five minutes if you can. Then breathe. Inhale to the count of four, and exhale to the count of four. As you do this breathing exercise, try to clear your brain of all the chatter. It may take awhile to calm your thoughts, but keep up the breathing exercise. The goal is to relax your thoughts to give your mind, soul, and body a chance to refresh and regroup. If you have the time to add more minutes, take advantage of it. These short breaks aren't time eaters. They'll actually add more time to your day by giving you more energy for how you use your time. This is called time efficiency.

Take advantage of every opportunity to pace your day. Get refreshed. Give yourself breathing space, putting distance between you and your tasks. Taking a few short breaks throughout a typical day adds more vitality, creativity, and sanity to an otherwise fast-paced, hectic, and drive-you-mad kind of day.

Never miss a break. In some states it is an employment law that workers get a fifteen-minute break after two hours of work. I can hear your thoughts about not having the luxury for breaks, because I've shared them as well. I've worked through breaks and wondered why I was exhausted. I finally realized that these breaks were necessary to pace my energy and concentration. If I couldn't afford a fifteen-minute break, I'd settle for ten or occasionally five. A very short break is better than none at all.

Are you so busy that you tend to skip meals? Taking a break to nourish our bodies is important for our minds as well. Since our body's cells are hardwired for survival, going too long without eating will switch our bodies into survival mode. It will send us on a quest for food. Skipping a meal actually makes us feel hungrier when the next meal rolls around. A couple of side effects from hunger that impacts our mental state are these:

- Decreased energy
- Decreased performance
- Mood swings
- Fatigue

Our bodies require three to five meals per day. Food is the fuel that provides us with vitamins and minerals. Make a sound choice to help your body serve you at its best capacity. My mother often scolded me about skipping meals during the years I suffered with anorexia. She said, "If you don't feed your car with gasoline, it won't operate at all. You've got to put gas in the car if you want it to run." This was her offering of sound instruction. I offer the same advice to you: you only have one body—please take care of it so that you can always be at your best.

Don't take lunch at your desk. Speaking of not skipping meals, when you take a lunch break, make it an enjoyable one. Sometimes we eat through lunch to meet a deadline, and this is permissible, but we shouldn't make it a habit. I used to eat at my desk and work through breaks. By the end of the day, I practically crawled to my car. Sometimes I was so tired that I'd struggle to stay awake while driving home.

During a lunch break, make a commitment to get away from your desk, even if it's just outside the building. Never make a practice of eating lunch in your office, because too often someone will stop by and talk shop. Remember, you deserve to get refreshed.

Create a Family/Fun Bulletin Board

If you have wall space by your desk, consider putting up a bulletin board and tacking all kinds of pictures on it. I have one just to the left of my computer monitor that holds pictures of family, pets, and friends—all of them happy and full of love. I also post my favorite sayings with words of encouragement and motivation.

When I find myself in a pickle, I lean back in my chair and survey my bulletin board. I'm surrounded with people whom I love and who love me, and I'm reminded that life is good because of the wonderful people who are part of me. I'm also encouraged by inspirational sayings that remind me of truth, peace, and joy. You know, life doesn't get any better than that!

Freshen Up at the End of a Work Day

One woman at my work always reapplied her makeup just before clocking out. She would swipe on lipstick, touch up her blush, add a few strokes of mascara, and freshen her breath with a mint. One day I asked her why she went through this routine. She said that her husband picked her up after work, and she wanted to be as pretty as she could for him.

Several days later when I had a few minutes to spare at the end of a work day, I decided to freshen up for my family. When I walked into the house, instead of the usual monotone "Hi, Mom," my kids all said, "Wow! Mom, you look great!" I learned something important that day: when Mama looks good, everybody feels good.

Listen to Your Body

Our bodies send us clear signals when they're tired and used up, although it's tough for us to recognize these signs when we're living in the fast lane. But think for a moment: how does your body try to attract your attention? Through insomnia? Headaches? Stomachaches? Loss of appetite? If you refuse to listen to these warnings, a bout of the flu that you might not be able to shake could begin to plague you. Or chronic fatigue may haunt you. Do yourself a favor—a huge favor. Turn up the volume, and listen to your body.

I've traveled through the school of hard knocks long enough to ratchet up the volume when my body tries to send me a message. I've learned that my body will have its way, so I might as well just listen. I must admit it was tough at first. But when I listened, it proved to be a wise decision. You may be thinking, *My job is demanding—I can't slow down until my project is completed.* You're not alone. But here's the begging question: what good will it be if you're sick while trying to meet a deadline? Why not take a few breaks to rest and renew?

Let's become an advocate for ourselves and listen to our bodies. They know when they need a timeout. When we respect our bodies, they respect us back. What can we do to keep our bodies healthy and happy? Here's an easy and logical plan:

- Eat healthy
- Hydrate
- Exercise
- Sleep well

When we eat right, engage in regular physical activity, and get plenty of rest, we will have the energy and resilience to deal with life's challenges.

My doctor asked me a series of questions during a recent annual physical exam. Her first question was whether or not I ate healthy. My answer: "Sure do! A muffin with six mugs of coffee to start my day."

After a short lecture on what healthy eating looks like came another question: "Do you exercise?"

I replied confidently, "Yes! I do one sit-up per day: at night I lie down in bed, and in the morning I sit up."

My doctor rolled her eyes and gave me another lecture. (Oh, please.) She asked if I slept well. My answer was simple: no. She gave me a prescription that no one in the fast lane wants to hear: go to bed at nine o'clock. I could read for an hour, but I was definitely to be in bed by nine.

I thought she was a bit nuts. In fact, she had lost me at the first question when she had told me that six mugs of coffee were four too many. Reluctantly I listened to the new "lights out" instruction, and within a few days I felt much better. Then I reduced my caffeine to two mugs and, wow! I felt so much better! It's important to listen not only to our bodies but to our doctors as well.

A friend of mine loves waxy chocolate donuts. He can consume an entire box at one sitting. Recently his doctor warned him to lay off sugar due to a borderline diabetic condition. Unfortunately, he is now diabetic and still eating those waxy icky donuts. His condition is a good warning to all of us: we should try not to get so attached to bad habits that we toss reason out the door.

Stay Alert

We cannot allow our days to run us. We must run our days. How? By staying alert to obsessive behavior—a trap we tend to fall into if we have high-demand jobs. We need to recognize when our passion is about to turn to poison.

The unanticipated outcome of working at high levels is that we set a standard for our accomplishment, for our day-to-day productivity, and high performance becomes an expectation. Instead of working to receive accolades, our own higher level becomes our norm, our standard. But when our passion turns to poison, we face burnout. We need to avoid the snare of burnout. If we want to raise the bar, we should do so with a consistent pace that will help us accomplish our workplace objectives while maintaining a lifestyle of balance.

Of course, staying on the leading edge is important, because that's what upper management looks for. But they also look for leadership, reliability, and loyalty. We don't have to kill ourselves to maintain these attributes, which ultimately speak louder than out-performing ourselves.

Start the Day with a Relaxing Ritual

Instead of jumping out of bed and getting dressed as soon as you wake up, try a different routine. Set your alarm to wake you up fifteen minutes earlier than usual, and use the extra time to set the tone and pace of your day. Try meditating, journaling, light exercising (stretching is wonderful to gently stimulate your body after a night's slumber), or reading something that inspires you. By doing these things, you give your brain and body advance notice on how it should behave throughout the day.

Set Boundaries

One of the things I learned while raising children is that kids need boundaries—a set of guidelines to live within. When they can trust these boundaries, they're more confident in who they are. Boundaries also apply to adults—you know, us big kids.

Don't overextend yourself. Learn to say no to requests for your time. If you find this difficult, remind yourself that saying no allows you to say yes to the things you truly want to do. If you're like me, I want to do everything, be involved with anything. But there's a downside to not setting boundaries: a stressed-out lifestyle.

Be Creative

We all have a creative bent in one way or another. You may say, "Yeah, I'm artistic all right. I can't even draw a straight line." Well, I can't either. But I can arrange flowers, stain glass, knit, and crochet. Here's the benefit of being creative: it escorts us away from a stressful life, albeit momentarily, giving us just enough time to take a break from life. When we return, we feel refreshed, and our perception of a problem or work project may be different after a short timeout.

Usually the things that cause us stress continue day after day for a period of time. But when we can put those things aside and become engrossed in a craft, we enjoy a sense of accomplishment.

Do Your Favorite Things

What are your favorite things to do? Whatever brings you joy will also give you hope. Make a list of your favorite things. Take a moment to ponder them, enjoy them, dream about them. When was the last time you thought about your favorite things? A long time, perhaps? Why not start enjoying them again today? Do something good for yourself—one of your favorite things. Return to what can energize you.

Conclusion

Stay in tune with yourself. Recognize the warning signs of impending burnout. If you don't address it, it will get worse. As you take steps to get your life back in balance, you can prevent burnout and avoid a full-blown breakdown.

Action Points

What areas in your lifestyle do you see as culprits that could cause burnout? Can you change them? How?

Identify a personality trait in you that is prone to burnout. What changes can you make to address this?

In what areas of your work life and home life could you serve yourself and others better if you paced yourself?

Have you turned up the volume to hear what your body is telling you about being overly stressed or burned out? What is it telling you to do?

Why is it important to stay alert to the possibility of obsessive behavior? What triggers have you identified that tell you that you may be on the brink of burnout?

One of the best rituals you can establish is beginning your day with a relaxing, introspective routine. What rituals will you incorporate at the beginning of each day?

People need to live within boundaries to remain in balance. What boundaries have you established?

Being creative can help you do something different, something you enjoy rather than stressing out about stressing out. What creative activity do you like to do, and when was the last time you did it?

What are your favorite activities? Will you plan to do one of these things today?

14

Guarding Your Life in a World of Demands

Twenty years from now you will be more disappointed by the things you didn't do than by the ones you did do. So throw off the bowlines. Sail away from the safe harbor. Catch the trade winds in your sails. Explore. Dream. Discover.

MARK TWAIN

Children can say whatever they think and get away with it. If adults made an inappropriate outburst, they would be chastised for it, even disrespected. But children don't let circumstances hinder them as we adults do.

I recently heard a joke about little Johnny and his family having Sunday dinner at his grandmother's house. Everyone sat around the table as the food was served. When little Johnny received his plate, he started eating right away.

"Johnny! Please wait until we say our prayer," said his mother.

"I don't need to," the boy replied.

"Of course you do," his mother insisted. "We always say a prayer before eating."

"That's at our house." Johnny explained. "But this is Grandma's house, and she knows how to cook."

As we adults face tough issues, we tend to stray from such childlike candidness. We stay silent when we feel trapped on an endless merry-go-round of busyness; when we suffer an injustice that hangs around our necks like a ball and chain because it may not be politically correct for us to speak up; when we're exhausted from giving and doing for others and become low on energy and time for ourselves. Busyness, suffering injustice silently, and exhaustion from endlessly giving and doing for others—do you see the common thread that binds all of them? Here it is: devoting more attention to others than to ourselves.

This thread can tangle us up, especially those of us who are fixers. By nature we're all fixers to some degree. Men tend to be fixers by virtue of their roles to protect and provide. Women are often fixers in the sense of being "teaspoon of sugar" types of nurturers. But when we spend too much time fixing others and not attending to our own need for balance, we become bogged down and start looking for ways to get off the merry-go-round of doing, doing, doing.

The Bible says that after creating the world God rested on the seventh day. What? God needed a day of rest? Or did he? Maybe he did this as an example for us humans. Surely he knew that we would run ourselves to exhaustion and wouldn't have the good sense to slow down. We live in a go-like-ninety culture in which we're expected to do more with less, live on the competitive edge, and be available at the beck and call of our families and employers. God knew all about the human dilemma and gave us a solution: rest at least one day a week.

One of my students had spread herself too thin while ignoring her own need for balance. Jamie had two small children and a husband, whose job took him on the road. She felt like a single parent, having to be both mom and dad. On top of this huge responsibility, she had a demanding job. One morning she glanced in the mirror and barely recognized herself. Her hair was stringy and dull. Swollen bags sat under her eyes like large brown pieces of luggage. She tried to look alert, but it required effort. She was spent. We all can feel like Jamie did when we're stretched too far. How can Jamie and the rest of us find the parts of ourselves that have been lost in the hubbub?

Let's take a good look at our lives through the lens of a few helpful tips that range from time management to finding our special place of respite. Then we will look at more introspective viewpoints of gratitude and faith—other attributes that can help us guard our lives and recapture anything we may have lost of ourselves as we have journeyed toward balance.

Manage Your Time

How well are you managing your time? If your response is, "I could do better," you're not the only one. When we think about how much time is available to us in a twenty-four-hour day, it's insane that we can't finish all our tasks.

One day when time was quickly slipping away, I wished for a twenty-six-hour day. All I needed was two extra little hours! But after thinking it over, I wondered if my bad habit patterns would carry over into those extra hours if I had them and I would squander them as well.

Such a dilemma.

Maybe a twenty-four-hour day was just right, I thought. Maybe more time would have found me spinning my wheels, leaving me more exhausted and frustrated. Maybe I needed to make an effort to organize my time and commit to becoming a better steward of what I had.

That's exactly what I did. My new focus helped me establish guidelines, which helped me tremendously. Here they are for you.

Count All Your Time

When we think about our day, we typically look at chunks of time: morning, noon, afternoon, evening. But our day doesn't consist of only chunks. Precious minutes tend to slip away unaccounted for. But because our moments are gone in a flash, we must account for *all* our time. "What does this mean?" I hear you asking. "Tracking every minute would be c-r-a-z-y!" But hold on! This is what I mean by tracking time: finding satisfaction out of every task.

In order to do this, I had to find a sweet spot—a motivator to keep me focused and diligent. See, when we approach a task with negative thoughts, we're naturally bogged down and uninterested in the job; this stale attitude causes us to take longer to complete a chore, and the result is that we squander our time. But I found my sweet spot for cleaning a bathroom, which is not my favorite thing to do. I do "war talk." While scrubbing a toilet, I say with gusto, "I'm at war! I'm killing germs! Filth be gone!" Before I know it, the chore is done, and I'm ready to tackle the next job—wiping down a million fingerprints on the stainless steel appliances in my kitchen.

Is there a task you're not fond of? How can you make the best of that chore? Create your own war talk, and notice how quickly you can get to the core of your tired attitude!

Create a To-Do List

In 1980 Harper House debuted its calendar organizer, the Day Runner. It became the most popular corporate daytime planner. I attended a four-hour workshop on how to use the handsome Day Runner, one of which my company had purchased for each of its managers. But I had one major problem: I didn't like the idea of taking orders from a piece of paper. Not only that, but I wondered how in the world I could possibly complete each item on my list in a given day. There just weren't enough hours! But I finally decided to buckle down and take orders from that piece of paper, and I was pleasantly surprised at how well my planner kept me focused and organized.

Then I learned another timesaving technique that the planner afforded me. At the end of each day, I looked over the notes I had written for the next day's schedule. This helped me plan the next day and set priorities.

Of course there were unexpected pop-ups as each new day progressed, but I learned to filter through them by asking,

- How urgent is this?
- Do I need to be flexible?
- Can I fit this in without unreasonably disrupting my entire day?
- Can I negotiate another day that would work better?
- Is this new task that my client added to the project I'm already doing for him more important than the original job? Which of the projects would my client consider deferring?

I also stand by a mantra that has served me well: "An emergency on your part does not constitute an emergency on my part." Because someone else is unorganized and has created an emergency doesn't mean that we need to have one. It is good to be helpful, but we must do so responsibly.

Reschedule an Appointment

The boss has scheduled an all-hands meeting that conflicts with another meeting you have on your calendar. What's the best way to reschedule your first meeting? Simply offer the person you were going to meet with two alternative dates. If you offer more, it will easily get out of control, and both parties will waste time and energy trying to decide on a date.

After I've offered two alternative dates, I lightly pencil them on my calendar. This way if something else comes up, I know that I have a tentative engagement already scheduled. Once the new date and time are definitely decided, I retrace the chosen penciled entry as a firm commitment and erase the other option.

Some people like a lot of choices, but when it comes to time management, less is more.

Keep Your Schedule Under a Microscope

Once time is lost, it can never be retrieved. It is helpful, therefore, to examine any bad habits that interfere with good time management. Be critical, honest, and thorough in your assessment of yourself. Identify those habits, and search for ways to change or eliminate them.

I look ahead at my commitments during the month. This review helps me remember upcoming appointments and due dates, and it provides me with enough time to plan and prepare for them. Looking at time under a microscope better organizes our days. That's empowering!

Concentrate on One Thing at a Time

Sometimes we must overlap or multitask to get things done, but when we do this, how productive are we? Do we make mistakes by doing two, okay, four things at once? What's our stress level? It's extremely helpful if we can learn to concentrate on one thing at a time.

Most of us have heard the saying, "The faster I go, the behinder I get." The key to overcoming this frustration is to focus and then execute. When we do this, we are able to see the whole task and organize our time better from a larger frame of reference.

On one particularly busy work day, I rushed to attend meetings and run errands. When I stopped at the post office to gather mail from my box, I was thinking about my next task and the best way to approach it. I hurried back to my car, tossed the mail into the backseat, and slammed the door shut.

Big problem. Somehow my finger got in the way.

I quickly opened the door and released my throbbing finger. I leaned back in the driver's seat, feeling the agonizing pain dart all over my body. I gritted my teeth while massaging my finger and saying bad things to myself. You know, the usual: "Dummy! Instead of nursing your smashed finger, you could be working on your next task! You're a big dummy!"

But sometimes interruptions can be profitable.

With this one I discovered something. While nursing my injured finger, I noticed that nothing else was important. Not the to-do list. Not rushing around. Not thinking ahead. While trying to massage the pain out of my finger, I decided to tackle each job one at a time—no rushing, just focusing. And guess what? I accomplished everything on my list—stress free and without any more smashed fingers! The end result was that an ugly day turned into a beautiful day!

Deal with the Dreaded *P* Word

The dreaded *P* word is "Procrastination" with a capital *P*.

We've all procrastinated. We need to get busy on a task, but suddenly we need to use the bathroom. Have a cup of coffee. Get something to eat. When we catch ourselves procrastinating, we should ask, "What am I avoiding?"

Maybe you've taken on a project that started small but grew into a mountain. But any task can be sectioned into smaller pieces, thus bringing manageability to an assignment. My grandmother always said, "What you can do today, do today." That's good advice. Taking care of business today means becoming responsible and being a better steward of your time. After all, who of us wants a task hanging around like a monkey on our backs? Why would we want to make our burdens heavier? Why would we want to defer a task until tomorrow?

Don't let procrastination plague you. The more you do, the more discouraged you'll become. And the further away from success you'll be.

Delegate

No person is an island. We all belong to a team. We are each a member of a family, a group of friends, a church, a volunteer organization, a work team, or some group. We can't successfully deposit money into an account without the help of our bank or credit union team. We can't buy groceries without a cashier. We can't use our credit cards to buy gasoline without a team of IT folks who have skillfully created a program to process our cards.

Since we are surrounded by teams, why do we rely upon ourselves for nearly everything? Delegation of certain tasks not only helps us manage our time but also allows others to function in their team capacity.

Be careful not to delegate mundane tasks to your team. When you do, you minimize the effectiveness of those working with you. Rather, delegate tasks of substance and importance. When delegating tasks, put yourself in the other person's position. How would you feel if you were given a boring task? Dumped upon? No one wants to feel insignificant.

When our collegiate daughter came home for winter break, she helped me arrange Christmas dinner for eighteen people. Instead of having her prepare a dish, I had her fetch things: "Get me that large mixing bowl." "Wash this frying pan." "Do this, do that." She was my kitchen gopher, which helped me a lot, but it was demeaning to her. She finally told me, "Give me something I can do, and don't just treat me like a slave." Ouch! But she was right. She was far more capable than I was giving her credit for. I had to overcome the fact that I needed to be in control. Double ouch!

The important issue here is valuing others enough to allow them to make their own contribution, to become part of a team. This is far more rewarding than simply giving people minimal tasks.

Manage Your Time by Managing People

All kinds of people step in and out of our life paths. Some enhance our lives. Others, however, are a drain. They're always calling us with the same problems. Sure, it's easy to take on a false sense of responsibility and try to fix these people. Helping others is noble and admirable, after all. But what is the expense to our own time management? We're tied up doing everything for everybody else—giving pieces of ourselves away and finding no reserve for ourselves.

At first glance this line of thought seems selfish, but our priority should be to take care of ourselves; if we don't, we won't be of optimal use to others anyway.

As we seek to take proper care of ourselves, we must recognize that some people will not be happy, no matter what we do for them, no matter how nice we are, no matter how much time and energy we give them. We need to face the fact that these people are not going to grasp the solution we've suggested to them again and again. If we find ourselves repeating the same suggestion, we need to ask these people, "Do you remember the answer we came up with for this problem?" Then let them own the previous conversation.

When we begin to feel as if we are a dumping ground for others, it's time we take a stand. But how can we do this when someone is hurting or really needs our advice? The key point here is not to be insensitive to the needs of truly hurting people but to set our own boundaries, because without them, other people will have license to bombard us. We don't need to be harsh or uncaring. But we need to be assertive and to understand that when we try to carry others' needs inappropriately, we're not being helpful. We do people a disservice when we allow them to use us as a crutch. People need to learn to stand on their own. Some experts call this tough love. It puts consequence where it belongs—with the decision maker. Many times giving a problem back to the other person is the most loving thing we can do.

Evaluate Your Progress

Remember the old saying "A stitch in time saves nine"? Being responsible for our time is that stitch that can save time and energy. One of the key components to time management is to make a habit of evaluating our progress. Let's say it's eleven o'clock and we've been working since eight. We should take a moment to check how we've used those three hours. Are we on schedule? Did we spend more time on a particular assignment than we had planned? Can we trim time from another task without consequence? Could interruptions have been better controlled? We should be sure to evaluate our progress at the end of the day too, asking the same questions we did in the morning.

What about those days when all our good intentions fall into a dark hole? We walk into the office and the phone rings with an emergency we must attend to. To make matters worse, this is followed by another unplanned assignment. At the end of the day, we didn't accomplish anything we had planned. A particular tip has helped me enjoy a bit of control over even these kinds of days: regardless of the time of day, try to start one item on the to-do list. Even if we don't finish it, at least we can say that we worked on our list! That's a good feeling.

Create Breathing Space

How many times have we been faced with an incredibly demanding day in which we don't seem to have time to eat, think, or even breathe? That's when we should create a relaxing place. I call it breathing space. This is an important part of time management.

I recently tried to create one minute of breathing space every hour during a highly demanding day. I did well the first hour but didn't stick with my plan throughout the day. Discouraged, I gave it up altogether.

Then the light bulb flashed! Why not set a timer? Many phones are equipped with a timer. If my timer sounded and I wasn't at a good stopping point, I continued working, but once I was at a place that allowed for a break, I took it. Taking a break—if only for a minute—helps us refocus, refresh, and recharge. And in the long run, it allows us to get more accomplished.

When relaxing in our breathing space, it helps to become conscious of our breathing. Are we taking short, staccato breaths or deep-down-to-our-toes kinds of breaths? In chapter 13 we talked about a five-minute breathing break, but other breathing exercises are as effective. Here's another type you might like to use: focus on filling yourself with deeper breaths. Get into a breathing rhythm: start with a long inhale, momentarily hold your breath, then end with a long exhale. Repeat this until you are breathing deeply. Close your eyes during this exercise, as then you'll get the optimum benefit by avoiding any possible distractions.

Cultivate Gratitude

Even in our most hectic moments, we can take a step back and be grateful.

I was recently teaching a course in the Midwest, had another class to teach the following week in California, had just picked up another huge project, and had calls coming in from a group for a China assignment. On the same day I received a call from a potential new client. I felt like an octopus with all my legs being tugged and pulled.

Overwhelmed, I took a step back and turned my anxiety into gratitude, focusing on being thankful for my building workload. Being thankful helped me gravitate to my place of center, and I was able to remember my purpose and avoid feeling overwhelmed by requests from others. It changed my short, rapid breaths to long, relaxing, calm ones.

Employ Faith

Finally, when the demands of others or the injustices of life threaten to get the best of us, we can employ faith. An old hymn goes like this: "Nothing is impossible when you put your trust in God. . . . Put your trust in God alone and rest upon his Word, for everything,

O everything, yes, everything is possible with God."[1] Trust means to let go and let God. When we do, our burdens no longer belong to us, and we can enjoy the journeys of our experiences.

Faith is especially helpful in helping us sift through our messes and find a nugget of gratitude amid our pressure or the strength to forgive those who are asking too much of us. During times when I've been knee deep in frustration, I have taken a step back and reached deep into my faith, where I can see more clearly, and I was then able to return to my climb with ease and confidence.

Conclusion

Discipline yourself to stay on task and honor your time-management plan. You'll be more confident in your judgment of priorities because you'll be determined to stick to them. Others will recognize your determination and respect you for it. You'll become a more reliable and trusted team member. When we can harness our time and use it efficiently, we'll protect ourselves from the inevitable demands that will be made upon our resources.

Make a commitment to incorporate time management, gratitude, and faith. Find your breathing space, your recharge. Give yourself a chance to reconnect so that you can be propelled toward your destiny.

Action Points

Life can grow into a monster and make you feel entrapped and unfulfilled. That's not the way God intends for you to live. His plan for you is purpose, accountability, and a disciplined lifestyle. When you live a focused life, you will be much happier. Take an assessment of the pieces of yourself that you may have lost in an effort to meet others' needs, and search for ways to make yourself whole.

People are typically fixers by nature. Recall a time when you "fixed" someone's problem over and over again. In other words, you took on a task that really didn't belong to you. In hindsight, what would you have done differently?

How can you create a plan to manage your time better?

When was the last time you examined your time—how you spent your day? Take a few minutes to assess your yesterday. What could you have done differently? Did you employ a good time-management habit that you would like to continue?

Do you tend to procrastinate? What are you trying to avoid?

Managing people in your life helps you manage your time. What would you say to someone who keeps seeking your advice for the same problem?

When you're working a particular task, have you thought about how you might save time? How you might be more efficient in decision making or anticipating roadblocks? Jot down a few notes here to make yourself more aware of how you might save time.

This chapter discussed creating breathing space, maintaining gratitude, and employing faith as ways to rediscover yourself and redeem what you may have lost of yourself. What was your takeaway from these sections?

15

Where Is Your Compass Pointing?

Whatever our wandering, our happiness will always be found within a narrow compass, and in the middle of the objects more immediately within our reach.

EDWARD G. BULWER-LYTTON

Someone started an argument with you. Your first reaction was to become angry, but you chose the higher ground. You stayed positive even though your heart was hurt and disappointed.

When we're on the right path, life is grand. We're productive, satisfied, confident. We're able to deal with stressors because our life is in balance. But sometimes we find ourselves distracted. When we stray off course, we become dissatisfied, unsure, and frustrated.

As the temptations and pressures of the world entice us to step in various directions, staying centered on our principles and goals is not always easy. That's the time we need to rely on a moral compass as a guide—on our true-north principles that form our beliefs, values, and convictions.

True-north principles are the natural laws of human conscience. These laws are timeless. They are inscribed in our hearts and stand at the ready to keep our compass pointing toward true north. The Bible tells us that God himself has written them on our hearts.

Why did he choose the heart and not the mind? Well, if you have a fickle mind like mine, it changes with the slightest breeze, and very little sticks to it. But the values nestled in our hearts are sure, personal, and committed. Holding fast to our true-north principles and living according to them, even when life gets crazy, is the surest way to find center and to maintain a balanced, happy life of purpose. Let's look at some of the principles that will hold us steady over the long haul and how we can implement them in our lives.

Integrity

One day in my first-grade catechism class, our teacher instructed us to open our coloring book for the day's lesson. Since I was a visual learner, this coloring book was my favorite part of class. The lessons depicted graphic messages through the large prints that drove their important guidelines straight to my six-year-old heart. That day's lesson was about choosing between good and evil, right and wrong.

On one side of the book, a wide, smooth pathway led to a destination that seemed to narrow farther along the path. It was a creepy picture, because Satan stood at the entrance of that easy-looking pathway with a sinister smile. On the other side of the book was a picture of a narrow path. That path was rocky and not appealing at all. But I liked the beautiful angel that stood at its entrance. Our teacher, a nun, explained that wide is the way of wrong decisions, but only the strong could survive the narrow and difficult path of right choices. I was drawn to the wide pathway; easy seemed best to my six-year-old reasoning. But my teacher spoke strongly against it, and that was warning enough for me. Even today, whenever

I'm faced with a choice between doing the wrong thing or the right thing, I'm returned in my memory to that coloring book and the convincing words of my teacher.

We've all been there—standing at a fork in the road, facing a choice between right and wrong. It may be a critical moment in our lives when we're encountering a life-changing decision. The right path may be the rockier road; it is narrow and steep, riddled with potholes. Yet anxious to make a choice, we quickly glance to the wrong way. We admire its level and wide path; it's a welcoming road. We ponder. The wrong road looks so easy. But something deep within us struggles for higher ground. That's integrity at work. It helps us be true to ourselves, even when we have to choose the toughest path.

Another facet of integrity is taking an honest look at ourselves and realizing that we are enough. In other words, that we've got what it takes to handle any situation—wisdom enough to guide others; laughter enough to help others discover humor in their situations; tears enough to help others dry theirs. The Bible says that we are equipped with inner strength to tackle any situation. God provides us all we need to be more than conquerors not only for our day but for a day in someone else's life too.

Fairness

At some time or other over the course of our lives, most of us have felt that something was unfair. But how do we really know what's fair or unfair? The best way to analyze the principles of justice is to ask some basic questions: Did a perceived injustice involve lying or taking advantage of others? Did it involve playing by the rules, or was it more about playing favorites? It can be difficult to stay objective when our emotions are concerned. The key is not to blame others for our own mistakes or deficiencies.

The most common tales of unfairness typically arise from siblings and how they view favoritism. "Mommy likes you best," a child blurts out through his tears. "Daddy never lets me go first." On and on the grievances are expressed as unjust treatment. But what we suffer as a child, if not dealt with, will follow us to adulthood. We will perceive the same types of unfairness, except that as adults, our problems will be more complicated. When an adult frets about unfair pay treatment, being passed over for a promotion, or supervisor favoritism, it's because he or she has been hit harder by the wounds of inequality. The injustice penetrates deeper because of bruises from childhood.

Unfairness tips us off center, and in our faulty attempts to correct the imbalance, we can interfere with our compass setting. Ever carry a large bag of groceries from the car to the kitchen? Have you noticed how heavy it seems to have gotten by the time you reach the kitchen? That's what happens when we carry the weight of unfairness—the burden gets heavier and heavier. We end up exhausted and off balance, because we have tried to force our compass in the right direction.

That's where we mess up. Why? Because we rely upon what we perceive as our best judgment. Let's make a vow to put aside the things we deem unfair and step into faith, knowing that God has a plan in the unjust situations in our lives. His plan is always in our best interest. If we let go of a wrong, God will make sure our compass readings are set in the right direction.

We all know that life isn't fair. Stuff hits the fan, spreading its toxins over everything and everybody. What's at the root of unfairness? Perhaps it has to do with our expectations. Have we set our sights too high? If we have, is life really unfair? A child sees his sister getting more attention than he is. He expects what she is getting. He doesn't get it and decides that Mommy likes his sister better. When we acknowledge our expectations, we're better prepared to be more realistic and avoid disappointments.

Kill 'em with Kindness

How do you feel when someone shows you kindness? Perhaps someone has given you a calming word during a heated exchange. A gentle voice can transform the direction of a conversation. If a person is feeling defensive and expecting a conflict, a gentle word can help usher that person to a better frame of mind. A kind word or gesture can even soothe an angry heart.

As a child, when I was hurt by others, my mother would tell me, "Kill 'em with kindness." It was a crazy thought. I wanted to retaliate! But I took her advice and found that kindness actually worked.

There's a story in the Bible in which a man asks Jesus how many times he should forgive someone. Jesus tells him, "Seventy times seven." Seems odd, doesn't it? But let's think about this for a minute. Seventy times seven equals four hundred ninety. Guess by the four hundred ninety-first time, forgiveness and kindness become natural behavior.

Dignity

When we maintain dignity, we convey human rights, common good, and respect for others. But another side of dignity is more introspective. For example, it is expressed in self-respect, self-esteem, personal poise, and pride. When our compass points to these qualities, we are then equipped to project dignity onto others. And when we're able to do that, we give away the very best of ourselves, which is the very least others deserve.

We must keep our trajectories pointed to this simple principle: we should treat others as we want to be treated. When we do this, we will be positioned to align ourselves with those who share similar values.

Why is this important?

In the early 1980s a new concept infiltrated the education system and corporate America. It was the principle of needing a village. For education the theme was "It takes a village to raise a child." In corporate America it was "Strong teams accomplish the impossible." The fact of the matter is, aligning with people who share our values strengthens us and encourages us to keep striving toward the abundant life God intends us to have.

People often seem to be strategically placed upon our life paths. The people we encounter either give us support and a strong sense of our true north, or they are difficult, and the rub of annoyance they bring us challenges us in our areas of weaknesses and causes us to be strengthened in character. Yes, these difficult people may be a royal pain, but I daresay we'll never forget them, because once we're able to forgive them, we will be able to see what a gift they've left for us.

Use Your Global Positioning System

GPS is a satellite-based navigation system consisting of twenty-four satellites that orbit the earth about twelve thousand miles above us, make two complete orbits in less than twenty-four hours, and travel at speeds of approximately seven thousand miles per hour. Simply put, it consists of the big-eye-in-the-sky that spots where we are at any given time. Need directions? No problem. Just put your destination into a GPS receiver like Google Maps, and a friendly voice will instruct you along your route, providing estimated travel time, mileage, and ample notice for changing directions.

While the laws of nature are written on our hearts, it's our minds that process those laws and tell us how to live them out. Our minds are like a GPS, sending messages that orbit within our gut feeling, or our sense of intuition. This helps us navigate our lives toward peaceful balance. How we program our minds is of paramount importance if we want to reach our desired destination. We must set our bearings in the right direction—toward true north.

Get Your Bearings

Is your world fraying at the seams with the nagging threat of layoff? A manic work place? A floundering relationship? The pain of loss? Whatever challenges haunt you today, know that your internal true-north bearings will operate in your favor.

Our brains are in a constant search to find a state of well-being, to create a new normal, to make sense of the senseless. Our former life experiences have prepared us for the new challenges we face today. They have formed our character, strengthened us in our weaknesses, and groomed our self-esteem. Now we must stand on our true-north bearings and stay focused. The endurance we exhibit today will make way for a better tomorrow.

Recalculate When Needed

When we make a wrong turn in traffic, as all of us do, the friendly voice on our GPS device helpfully tells us that we need to "recalculate"—to rethink where we're going. It doesn't scold by saying, "You screwed up—again!" Like the gentle GPS guide, when we get off track in our journey toward abundant life, we should be kind to ourselves, because negative words are poison to our self-esteem.

So you've made a wrong turn. Forgive yourself for the mistake, and get back on track. Think positively. Speak only the good things that your mind hungers to hear. After all, our minds are working in our best interests—seeking to keep us balanced and living in healthy reality. Although we get frustrated with ourselves for making mistakes, on the flip side, we can learn invaluable lessons from those mistakes. Welcome them, knowing that a mistake today can be a promise for a successful tomorrow.

Conclusion

Are you where you're meant to be? Have you taken a detour from your purpose? We tend to get distracted by the alluring thought that the grass is greener on the other side of the fence, but the hands that engineered your life path have also positioned your true north with plans to prosper you, not to harm you; plans to give you a hope and a future.

Like the GPS, your true-north principles will let you know when your pace lags or when you've traveled off course. The steps you take today toward a life of balance may seem unsure, foreign, even frightening, but if you keep moving toward true north, you will never be led astray. All you need to do is trust the next step.

For me, my GPS is the unconditional love of God, who has a plan for my future. His plan to prosper me and not to harm me is a promise that keeps me at true north. When I seek him, he meets me—not at his level but at mine. I've had many moments of knowing God's presence in my life, and each one has been an unspeakable and humbling experience.

Find your compass, and watch the needle automatically point to your true north. Your personal compass will provide markers to alert you to the hazards along the way. When you follow it, you'll stay centered and won't fall prey to distractions and unwanted influences. We all have a tendency to try to maintain control over our lives, but if we go with the flow and trust the path before us, we will be able to keep focused and stay on track on our way to a life of balance.

Action Points

This chapter discussed the major role integrity plays when people take an honest look at themselves. Take a moment to look at yourself through the eyes of integrity. Jot down what you see. Remember to write only positive observations.

Expectations are a huge part of how people set standards in their personal space. Sometimes they set them too high, and they end up disappointed when they see all the unfairness around them. Have you set an unrealistic expectation? If so, document it here, and decide how you can reestablish it with more realistic parameters.

No doubt many people have grown up with the Golden Rule—to treat others as one would like to be treated. One of the toughest things to do is to return kindness for an offense. Have you had an experience with someone in this regard that you'd like to rethink? How would you have treated that person if you had used a gesture of kindness?

Your mind is like a GPS, constantly sending you messages that help you navigate your life. Has your mind ever sent you a message that led you down a wrong path? How did you recalculate?

Name at least three ways you can keep your compass at true north.
1.
2.
3.

16

Maintaining a Balanced Life

For every minute you are angry, you lose sixty seconds of happiness.

RALPH WALDO EMERSON

So you want to live a balanced life. And you're brave enough to do something about it. You've decided to take responsibility for your own happiness, set some life goals, and begin your climb toward a you-phoria state of mind. But despite your best intentions and honest efforts, life will still throw a wrench in the works from time to time. How can you maintain the life of balance you desire to live on a consistent basis?

This desire we have to live in center is actually regulated by our brains. The human brain seeks a constant state of balance, and when that balance is disturbed, the brain generates a great deal of energy to get back in balance.

But let's face it—when we're going through a challenge, the last thing we want to do is *wait* for our brain to get its act together. We grow uncomfortable when we're not in balance, and our impatience triggers us to take charge and fix things, make them better, grab a solution—even though our plans may not be well thought out. Sound familiar? Well, you're not alone!

When we take control, we're barking up the wrong tree. We do ourselves a huge favor when we let go. Being out of balance is an opportunity for us to let God take over. This is exactly what God invites us to do when we get off balance—to cast all our cares upon him.

The word "cast" is interesting. It reminds me of the sport of fishing. One method of fishing is to throw the fishing line out as far as possible; this is casting the line. The same concept applies to throwing our cares as far as we can. When we cast our problems upon God and entrust them to him, we free ourselves from sadness, anxiety, fear, frustration—all behaviors that prevent us from living in center.

In our quest to live centered lives, we need to relax and give our brains the time they need to get back to a balanced state. But while we wait for our brains to take action, there are methods we can apply to help us remain in center. The following helps will work differently for each individual's personality, but one or more may really fit your need. Let these ideas feed your sweet spot when it comes to your own ambition and need. May you find yourself soaring like an eagle as you voyage through the changing winds that will lead you closer to your special place of center.

Live in the Moment

True living is always *now*. It's not regretting the past—that's already gone; wave good-bye to it. It's not worrying about the future—who can anticipate what might or might not happen tomorrow? Rather, awaken your heart to this very moment.

Approach this moment with an alert mind. Do whatever it takes to forbid thoughts from the past and about the future to intrude into your moment. Allow only "right now" thoughts. Ask yourself, "What do I know right now?" and then listen to the gentle whisper of the moment.

If you're experiencing a financial dilemma, for example, let your moment make an assessment. It may say, "Right now the refrigerator is full—you will not starve. Right now the utilities are paid—the fridge will remain cold. Right now life is good." This is your moment of discovery—staying focused on the positive things in your life. Right now.

Live in Gratitude

It's really tough to be depressed and grateful at the same time. When we welcome the moment—what we know for sure right now—we can embrace it with gratitude. Recognizing what we have in the moment and identifying all those positive things will automatically escort us to a place of thanksgiving. This is about counting our blessings.

Try this simple drill: based upon your awareness of your current moment, think of three things to be thankful for, and express your thanks out loud. Here are a few examples: "I'm thankful that my fridge is full. I'm thankful that my utilities are paid. I'm thankful that I'm okay." And you *will* be okay in the next moment—and in the moments after that!

Practice an attitude of gratitude—make it a habit. Living in gratitude is accepting responsibility for our own well-being.

Live in Integrity

When we do what's right, we perform at our optimum. Living in integrity produces courage and contented well-being in our lives. But here's the grand prize of integrity: it will never fail us. Doing the right thing, even if it's the hardest thing to do, will always be rewarded in one way or another.

So when you face tough choices, follow your true-north principles, and do what is right. If you take the first step in maintaining integrity and honor as you walk through difficult situations, God will give you the strength for your journey toward abundant life. And when you do the right thing, don't let it go unrecognized. Validate your accomplishment by telling yourself, "Good job!" Always reinforce the behavior you want to see in yourself. A life of integrity may require a steep climb, but the reward is discovering higher ground.

Live in Happiness

Our bodies and minds weren't designed to live with the aggravation of worry. Rather, we are called to realize our potential and become alive with happiness. Sometimes, however, we get tangled in stress, and worry robs our joy. What's the fix? We need to work on our moods. Happiness is something we prepare for mentally. So set your mind in the right direction. That means waking in the morning determined to have a good day. It means putting on the garment of joy and shedding the heaviness of life. When there seems to be no way, joy paves the way for hope, and joy becomes our strength.

When I have dealt with an issue during happy times and the same issue while I was preoccupied and anxious, I have found the contrast in my responses to be an eye opener. When we are happy, we see a problem from a healthy perspective. We don't take the problem as seriously as we would if we were unhappy. We don't sweat the little things or pick the problem apart. Because we are not tied up in knots with anxiety, we can think better and with more confidence. We also don't use up as much energy to solve a problem as we would if we were preoccupied and anxious.

Honestly, there's a world of difference between handling a problem from a happy point of view and doing so from an anxious, nervousness-riddled perspective. The latter complicates life so much more. And really, who wants that?

Live in Quality

How we manage our time will dictate the depth of our fulfillment and joy. Time shouldn't be defined as "quantity" but as "quality," which means getting the most value out of the least amount of time.

To do this we must stay focused on whatever task is at hand. Don't allow distracting thoughts or interruptions to compromise the quality of your time while playing with a child, coaching an employee, enjoying a good book. Time is irredeemable. We can't go back to yesterday to recoup time lost. We can manage, however, the time that we have, and we can ensure that it is spent in a quality way. Be a good steward of your time. Find your purpose for today, and live every minute of it with strong intention.

Live in Your Destiny Dream

Why is it important for us to reach our dreams, purposes, goals, and ambitions? Because God has planted dreams in our hearts, and as we feed the hunger of our purposes, we satisfy our natural needs for fulfillment. When we are satisfied and fulfilled, we find ourselves living in center.

A destiny dream is a desire, a longing to realize our purpose. Imagination ignites our destiny dreams, nourishes the seeds of our dreams, and helps them grow. Do you have a dream simmering inside you? A dream is not just a dream, though; it takes hard work. Today make a commitment to hunt for your destiny dream. Set your sights on growing your imagination, and embark on the path your heart is meant to chase after.

It takes a plan to keep a dream alive. Make a daily affirmation that kindles the fire of your dream. When your mind hears the repetitive affirmation of your dream, your dream will take form and become a reality.

At any time while traveling to your destiny dream, you may encounter the heaviness of discouragement. Don't cave in to its trappings to give up. Keep this important point in mind: on the other side of discouragement is the next level of growth and fulfillment. Allow faith to lift your head high, and work through the weight that tries to hold you down. Fight back! Tell discouragement that there are brighter days ahead. Remember your passion, that strong grip of enthusiasm that you had at the beginning of your dream. It still exists within you. Resurrect it; give it permission to carry you over the rough spots. Let the clouds part and the sky open up. Fill yourself with hope, confidence, expectation.

Make "dream" a verb. Put feet to your dream. Keep motivated, because motivation doesn't see roadblocks; it only sees possibilities. Keep climbing. Keep seeking. Keep trying. Be poised, ready to take a risk. Risk ushers us to discover new levels of accomplishment as we step outside our comfort zones. It is then that the right people will join our journeys to help nudge us forward.

Finally, be patient. It doesn't matter how quickly we get to our dreams. It matters that we keep moving.

Live in Fun and Laughter

When was the last time you laughed? I mean, when was the last time you really let hearty laughter rip from the depth of your being? Experts say that laughter is good medicine. It's a powerful antidote to stress, pain, and conflict.

Nothing works faster to bring our minds and bodies back into balance. Humor lightens our burdens, inspires hope, and connects us to others. It keeps us grounded, focused, and alert. With its power to heal and renew, laughter is a tremendous resource and supports both physical and emotional health. So what are some ways that we can bring laughter into our lives? The answer is quite simple—in fact, it's mind-bogglingly simple: smile!

Smiling is the beginning of laughter. The act displays positive body language and sends messages to our brains that happiness is within reach. Conversely, a grimace displays negative body language and sends unhappy signals to our brains.

Humor shifts perspective and allows us to see situations in a more realistic, less threatening light. So take a break and laugh! Hugh Sidey, an American journalist who worked for both *Life* and *Time* magazines, has said, "Carry laughter with you wherever you go."[1] That's wise advice!

Live in Twenty-Twenty Vision

We don't always see things as clearly as we should, but in order to remain in center, we need to have an accurate view of ourselves and of our circumstances. One way we can have this kind of twenty-twenty vision is to see ourselves as God sees us.

My mother recently had cataract surgery, and she was amazed at how well she could see afterward. She began boasting of twenty-twenty vision. But one thing was wrong: she could now see all the lines on her beautiful eighty-six-year-old face—and more. One day when I visited her shortly after her surgery, she raved about all the things she could now see. Then she suddenly leaned into me and looked over my face. With much concern, she said to me, "Carol, look at all the lines on your face." I pulled away, hoping the distance might dim her new keen vision. "I'm glad you have clearer vision," I told her, "but haven't you made enough observations for one day?"

Our pictures of reality when it comes to ourselves and our circumstances are stored in our subconscious minds, and, like gravity, our minds pull us to those pictures. To attract ourselves to the right picture, one of the best things we can do is to see ourselves as God sees us—and he sees us blessed, prosperous, talented, successful.

But not all of us see ourselves as God sees us, and therefore we tend to make excuses in an effort to minimize our failures. Eighteenth-century English poet Alexander Pope has said, "An excuse is worse and more terrible than a lie, for an excuse is a lie guarded."[2] What lies are your excuses guarding? What weak areas at home or in your job performance do you feel compelled to create excuses for? If you don't like something about yourself, definitely take it out of your conversation—refuse to say anything negative about yourself. You want to be proud of everything you put in front of people. George Washington Carver, an American botanist and inventor, said something really fitting to this perspective: "Ninety-nine percent of all failures come from people who have a habit of making excuses."[3] Don't let the disappointments of your past limit your vision. Replace the picture you have of yourself with a picture of how God sees you.

You may be saying, "Hold on! I've tried countless times to change my image, my picture." We've all gone through this, but while doing so, did you keep an open mind? Don't let the blinders of a closed mind interfere with your vision. They will keep you from changing your picture, because the information you need will be stymied.

Here's another important point about maintaining twenty-twenty vision: the more we see, the more we'll want to see. Want a big life? Then enlarge your vision. You may not be sure how your dream will unfold, but when you enlarge your vision, you just know it will. Dream big! Change the picture! Instead of just having a dream, you'll be living your dream.

Conclusion

Living joyously in center is about being alert to what's happening in our lives *right now*. Exercise only the twenty-twenty vision that leads you to become all you can be in the moment in which you are living.

Living in center is not a cookie-cutter lifestyle. There is no one panacea for everyone. Rather, each of our journeys is uniquely designed and can come in as many shapes and sizes as there are human personalities, needs, wants, desires, concerns, and issues. Letting go and letting God is critical to living in center and enlarging our unique visions.

If you want to live in a state of you-phoria with the confidence to journey into uncharted territory, take a leap of faith, and give yourself permission to explore the unknown aspects of your life. Allow the real you to be built in character. As you do, you'll recognize your own place of center more easily and consistently—and then you'll be ready to live in increasing fullness and harmony. Most importantly, you'll be able to live the life God has always planned for you.

Keep learning. Keep listening. Keep growing with the love of the divine God.

Action Points

You have the power to live a balanced life. No one can take that away from you. Set the fire ablaze in your heart to live a centered and joyous life today.

This chapter offered several tips for living in center. Did one or more of them resonate with you? If so, take a few minutes as we come to the end of the book and the final action points to write out affirmations that fit your unique needs.

Living in the moment:

Living in gratitude:

Living in integrity:

Living in happiness:

Living in quality:

Living in your destiny dream:

Living in fun and laughter:

Living in twenty-twenty vision:

Appendix 1

Erik Erikson's Life Stages

Life Stage	Conflict	Outcome/ Strength	Significance
1. Infancy: birth to 18 months	Trust vs. mistrust	Drive, hope	The quality of care given to the helpless infant determines whether the child will learn to trust and subsequently have hope.
2. Early childhood: 18 months to 3 years	Autonomy vs. shame	Self-control, courage, will	Learning to walk and talk brings independence and opportunity to build self-esteem.
3. Play: 3–5 years	Initiative vs. guilt	Purpose	A young child mimics adults in play in what is called social role identification; if the child is frustrated in natural desires, he or she can develop feelings of guilt rather than growing in personal initiative.
4. School age: 6–12 years	Industry vs. inferiority	Method, competence	A child learns and creates new skills at this stage of development. Unresolved feelings of inadequacy and inferiority can lead to serious problems in terms of competence and self-esteem.

Erik Erikson's Life Stages *Continued*

Life Stage	Conflict	Outcome/ Strength	Significance
5. Adolescence: 12–18 years	Identity vs. role confusion	Devotion, fidelity	An adolescent being neither a child nor an adult, life becomes complex as a young person attempts to find his or her own identity, struggle with social interactions, and grapple with moral issues.
6. Young adult: 18–35 years	Intimacy and solidarity vs. isolation	Affiliation, love	A young adult seeks mutually satisfying relationship experiences and intimacy on a deep level. If not successful, he or she may develop isolation and distance from others and, in defense, can feel superior to others.
7. Middle adulthood: 35–55/65 years	Generativity vs. self-absorption or stagnation	Production, care	A middle adult is at the age of self-actualization—realizing everything he or she has worked for. He or she faces midlife crisis—and struggles with finding new meaning and purpose. Difficulty with this stage can result in self-absorption and stagnation.
8. Late adulthood: 55/65–death	Integrity vs. despair	Wisdom	A satisfied older adult looks back on his or her life with happiness and contentment, with a deep sense that life has meaning and that he or she has made a contribution to life. A dissatisfied older adult despairs at his or her experiences and perceived failures. He or she may fear death in the struggle to find purpose in life.

Appendix 2

Tony Robbins's Concept of Need

Certainty. To be secure—to know what to expect and how to survive—we need to be comfortable, pleased, and not in pain, hungry, or tired. We need to have people and environments we can count on to help us when we run into trouble. Because each of us is different and comes from different life experiences, what makes one person feel secure will differ from that of others. That goes for all needs at this level. For example, for you security may come only after you have a million dollars in the bank; someone else may need only a warm meal every day.

Variety. We don't want to be stuck in a routine. We need creativity, a little uncertainty, a little excitement. We need some kind of challenge in our lives to help us grow mentally and physically. Again, the means of satisfying our needs will differ. You may enjoy hang gliding; someone is challenged by watching action movies.

Self-esteem/significance. Everyone desires to feel important, needed, wanted, and esteemed. We compete with each other to see who can be the most significant; even siblings vie for parental attention. Building self-esteem is tricky, because we do not always gain it in a healthy way. For example, some people gain it through destruction and by taking control of all the power.

Relationship. We need to love and connect with others. This need is at our core—even as infants we are receptive to it. We desire to be touched and to touch others, both emotionally and physically. Even those who do not experience romantic love can find ways to satisfy themselves by maintaining connection with their communities or their workplaces.

Growth. It is a universal truth that everything is either growing or dying. If we want to become better, improve ourselves, stretch and excel, we must cultivate this desire in order to grow. This need is hard to provide for, especially if we desire to provide it for others, because our requirements regarding growth change as we age and progress through the various life stages.

Contribution. This need is the hardest of all to meet, because it requires moving beyond our own pain and need and focusing on the needs of others. Once we are sure that we ourselves are surviving and thriving, it is important that we connect with others and contribute to their satisfaction.

Appendix 3

Personal Accountability Techniques

Having accountability means being responsible to set goals and achieve them. Maintaining personal accountability will not only help you reach the goals you aspire to, but it will improve your character and enable you to pass character on to those you love as well.

Whatever you put into personal accountability is what you'll get out of it; hard work leads to good results. Conversely, if you look for the easy road and reject accountability, you'll end up with clutter in your life that will keep you from living abundantly. This appendix lists a number of ways that can help you remain accountable to work hard and accomplish the goals you have set in your life.

Create Goal Cards

Documenting your accountability goals ensures that you will steadily progress toward their achievement. Doing this is helpful for

- Defining your goals
- Creating a plan to meet your goals
- Executing your plan to achieve your goals

Writing out your goals will give you a good reminder of them. It will help you become centered and focused on creating good habits and self-discipline as you seek to live out a balanced and productive life.

Gather a stack of three-by-five index cards, a pen, a highlighter, and a card-file box of your choice. I recommend a file box equipped with tabbed separators, as it will facilitate organization and easy access to specific topics. Once you have collected these things, use your index cards to create categorized lists of goals. This is what one of my cards looks like:

Date	Goals
_____	Create business website (completed 7-17)
_____	Keep current on "Back to Basics" bi-monthly contribution to *ROW* magazine
_____	Increase training schedule by two courses per year as of 2013. Current count eighteen courses per year. (Exceeded by six classes—yay!)
_____	Keep current on Cornerstone's to-do list for writing projects: first quarter, second quarter, third quarter, fourth quarter
_____	Get more rest to relieve stress—doc says bed by nine
_____	Read self-help books—thirty pages per day
_____	Write at least four pages per day

Note 1: Highlight goals once you have accomplished them. It's a helpful way to track what you've done.

Note 2: Decorate your index-card box, or purchase a decorative one at a stationery store.

Review Your Goals Often

Once you have identified and written down your goals, it is important to review them regularly. Reviewing your goals once a month isn't quite enough. To stay at the top of your game, try to review them at least once a week. When you first write out your goals, it sets your compass, your focus. Each time you review your goals, you reset your compass. With all the sundry distractions that can rob us of progress, a weekly review is a must.

Accountability goal cards track our progress and are a constant reminder to us of our plans to improve our lives. At times one goal will stand out more than another, and then that goal needs more thought, more prayer, more analysis. During the course of a day, as we are alert to what needs to happen to make that goal a reality, almost invariably information will come across our paths that will lead us to achieving that goal.

When you have a day that turns into a time robber, it helps to remove your current goal card from your index-card box and keep it in a conspicuous place on your desk or someplace where you can see it at an easy glance throughout the day. This kind of constant reminder will help exercise your self-discipline muscle. At the end of the day, you will have accomplished important tasks as they relate to your goals—rather than just having spun your wheels and caved into distractions.

Self-discipline has a way of expanding its boundaries. For example, when we're disciplined in one area, it affects other areas in our lives. Thus our personal accountability cards help us in many areas of our lives.

Grow Your Character to Reach Your Goals

In order for us to accomplish goals, we must exercise certain character traits. For example, you set a career goal for a promotion. You work really hard, but a promotion doesn't happen. Why? Could it be that one or two of your character attributes are out of sync with your goal? Could it be that you aren't disciplined enough, confident enough, or resourceful enough to get where you want to be?

Once you identify the character qualities you're missing, it's time to develop them. If your character and goals are incongruent, it will be tough to reach your goals. Examine a goal in which your progress has been disappointing. Now ask, "Is who I am right now sufficient to fulfill this goal? Am I assertive enough? Disciplined enough? Courageous enough? Flexible enough? Thankful enough? Motivated enough? Confident enough?" By taking a character inventory for each of your goals, you'll end up with a list of qualities to focus on. Knowing what character quality needs your attention will give you direction. The more you develop that character attribute, the closer you are to achieving your goal.

Remember, any character building that you accomplish now will serve you well later. Character qualities like self-esteem, self-discipline, gratitude, courage, and confidence pay dividends in all areas of life. Character building is an investment in *you*. Keep getting better. Never ever shortchange yourself.

Using your index cards to list character qualities you want to develop can help in the growth process. Here is an example of one of mine:

GRATITUDE ATTITUDE

I am thankful for . . .
- Birds chirping on this warm, sunny spring morning
- God always being faithful
- Positive feedback for magazine column; column voted number one by membership in 2013 survey
- Positive feedback from engagements
- Meeting a key contact in Atlanta, Georgia
- Lulu, the mini schnauzer we adopted
- Sleepovers with my grandchildren
- The pool being like bath water—ahhhh
- Receiving the highest education award from IRWA, Education Foundation, 2014

Build an Accountability Partnership

No person is an island. We should not behave as if we were. One of the best methods to achieving goals is to have an accountability partner—someone who can help you and whom you can help. Identify a friend or family member who can coach and encourage you to achieve your goal and whom you can encourage as well. Make sure that he or she has something in common with your goal and also has a healthy relationship with you. For example, if one of your goals is to lose weight, look for a friend who has an interest in exercise and health.

Once you identify your partner, decide on how frequently you should stay in contact with that person to discuss your goals and progress. Make plans on how you will stay in contact—e-mail, phone, a meeting for coffee. Make this aspect of your accountability regime as much fun as you can. This is a time to relax with a friend and enjoy camaraderie, support, encouragement, and even a few laughs.

As a partner, always start your discussions with praise. If your partner hasn't done well, look for anything positive and bring it to his or her attention. However, if the person has severely digressed and you can't find a speck of praise, then ask a series of questions to help your partner define his or her own path of commitment.

Frannie felt defeated after eating a lot of desserts at a baby shower. Fortunately, her partner looked for something positive to tell her. When she couldn't find one, she asked a question: "How many are 'a lot' of desserts?" With downcast eyes Frannie replied, "Three." Other questions, however, turned up the fact that Frannie had stuck with her diet on the other six days of the week. Now that was something to shout about! Way to go, Frannie!

After the praise comes a constructive critique. This should contain honest, candid, caring, and helpful suggestions. Our intention should be, "How best can I promote my friend? If I were in my friend's shoes, what would I need to hear?" As Frannie's accountability partner, we might ask her, "What could you do differently next week?" It is always best to provide guidance during this phase of the partnership and allow the other person to arrive at his or her own ideas of righting a wrong. Ask a series of questions, prompting the person to search deeper for what works best.

When your partner responds to a question, he or she may continue the answer with "but..." Help your partner avoid following up an answer with "but," because whatever comes after the "but" is the person's truest negative feelings. These feelings are a Band-Aid to the first part of the sentence. Here's an example—let's use Frannie again to make our point. She says, "I knew I shouldn't have had that second helping because it made the third so much easier, *but* I have such a sweet tooth." This is how our subconscious works with the trailing "but" statement: "I have a sweet tooth, therefore it must be satisfied." The more that "but" statement is fed (literally), the more Frannie will likely be to deviate from her diet.

Compose Affirmation Statements and Tag-Along Sentences

An affirmation statement is a powerful tool to help you accomplish your goals by creating positive statements to describe a desired situation or goal. For them to be successful, it will be helpful for you to recite the affirmation statements until they are impressed in your subconscious mind. This process causes the subconscious mind to work on your behalf to make the positive statement come true. That's why the affirmation statement must be composed of a thought that matches your goal and moves you forward.

Repeated positive statements will help you focus your mind on your aims. Here are a few ideas for getting the most out of repeating affirmations:

1. Choose affirmations that are not too long.
2. Repeat them every time the affirmation comes to mind.
3. Be as relaxed as you can.
4. Pay full attention to the words you are repeating.

5. Choose positive words with no negative connotations. If you want to lose weight, don't use words such as "I am not fat" or "I am losing weight." These are negative statements, bringing into the mind mental images of what you do not want. Repeat instead, "I am getting slim," or, "I have my ideal weight." Such words build positive images in your mind.
6. Affirm using the present tense, not the future tense. Saying "I will be rich" means that you intend to be rich one day or in the indefinite future but not now. It is more effective to say and also to feel, "I am rich now," and the subconscious mind will work in your best interest to make this happen now, in the present.

There's a pattern to each of these six ideas. Each one tells your subconscious mind something positive about the behavior it expects to see. When you follow these ideas, your actions, or behavior, will eventually catch up with your thoughts. You'll reap the benefits of a positive affirmation when your behavior automatically changes because of the thoughts you have programmed into your mind.

When filling out your goal cards, think about attaching a statement of affirmation that supports your effort to reach each goal. Compose a statement that will keep you focused, on task, running your race! Start the statement with, "It's not like me to _____." For example, if your goal is to exercise three times each week, your affirmation might be, "It's not like me to ignore a three-day exercise plan each week." Be sure to recite this affirmation several times each day and then watch your actions catch up with your thoughts. What affirmation could we recommend to Frannie? "It's not like me to have more than one dessert a week."

Be careful not to design an affirmation around the "but" statement. The "but" is an enabler. It says, "I have a sweet tooth, therefore I must satisfy it." Carefully design the affirmation statement around your goal, because the goal is the focus. You'll find that goal orientation dilutes the importance of the "but" statement.

Think about the affirmation statement as your A ("affirmation") game and the "but" statement as your B ("but") game. Your A game will help you focus on the behavior you want to grow. This is why it's important to highlight your goal and nothing else.

After you've created an affirmation statement, add a solid thought to it. This is a tag-along sentence of an implied thought. It's a follow-up thought, a reality-check statement. The tag-along attracts a deeper commitment.

This is how it works: Let's use Frannie's A game statement: "It's not like me to have more than one dessert a week." Her tag-along might be, "Because bingeing really frustrates me." The tag-along statement actually adds fuel to self-discipline. It will put you in the driver's seat and get you to the finish line of your goal. An affirmation statement and the implication of the tag-along will groom good behavior and strengthen your character. So bring on your A game!

Below is an example of some of my affirmations. I use my index cards for these as well:

AFFIRMATIONS and TAG-ALONG SENTENCES

It's not like me to . . .
- allow stress to dominate, because it robs me of my joy
- be unthankful, because God has blessed me—a lot!
- forget to exercise or take vitamins, because I need to be healthy for myself and others.
- be anal, because it's a waste of time and energy.
- be undisciplined in pursuing my goals, because God has a plan.
- write less than four pages a day on *Uncharted Territory*, because I'll never finish this book if I don't.
- read fewer than thirty pages a day of a self-help book or ignore my professional development, because personal enrichment helps me keep my work current and relevant.

Note 1: The affirmations I listed in the above example have to do with personal behaviors. I have other affirmations that relate specifically to my goals.

Note 2: It's handy to number the three-by-five cards in the upper right-hand corner. It's easier to keep track of the cards according to date.

Give Yourself Special Recognition

Recognition is celebration of an accomplishment. Why not celebrate yourself for being accountable, self-disciplined, and patient? Besides encouraging you, the power behind recognition will reinforce the behavior you want to continue seeing in yourself.

Some folks feel uneasy about celebrating themselves or bringing attention to their accomplishments. But it's not egotistical to give yourself some praise. Truth be known, we all have an invisible sign hanging from our necks saying, "Make me feel important." If you recognize your progress and believe in yourself, imagine what you can accomplish.

A celebratory event might be as simple as taking some time for yourself—to read, relax at the beach or the lake, or enjoy your favorite beverage. We can thrive a long time on a single recognition. Wouldn't your accountability partner love to celebrate with you too?!

Create a Memory Bank

Monitor your personal accountability progress by creating a memory bank. Track all the right things you've accomplished and deposit them into your memory bank. By doing this you won't let your hard work go to waste.

It's easy to create a memory bank by journaling your accomplishments. Success stories that are stored in your memory bank will serve as a foundation for you to stand upon during tough days. When things aren't going well, you'll need fuel to keep going, and your memory bank will be a reminder that what you've done before, you can do again! It will say, "You can stay strong, because you've been strong in the past."

For my memory bank I chose a journal with a luscious purple leather cover. With pen and my journal in hand, I find a quiet, cozy place to write about my successes. I write about my struggles as well so that the next time I'm at a tough spot, I can go back and read about how I overcame it and can remind myself of the strategy I used and how well it paid off. It's surprising how easily, in our busy lives, we can forget the events of our journeys. A memory bank can be your chronicle of the stories you experience as you navigate uncharted territory toward a balanced life.

Conclusion

Let the ideas in this appendix and the accompanying sample cards from my file box launch new ideas within you for building your own personal accountability techniques. Create accountability goals to fit your needs, and design your own cards to serve as tracking and motivation on becoming the best you ever!

Appendix 4

Creating a Mental Map

Take a sheet of paper, and fold it or draw on it to create four squares. Label each square as follows: at the top left write, "1. Goal"; at the top right write, "2. Self-sabotage"; at the bottom left write, "3. Anxiety"; and at the bottom right write, "4. What I know for sure." Then follow the instructions below to navigate this mental-map exercise.

1. *Goal.* Pick a goal, one that would lead to a significant difference in your life. It might be a New Year's resolution or a promise you've been making and breaking for years.
2. *Self-sabotage.* List all the ways you routinely sabotage yourself regarding this goal. If you're like me, I am gung ho on a goal for the first week. I track my progress daily and give myself high fives. But by the third week, the honeymoon is over, and I start to sabotage myself with procrastination. My go-to statement becomes "I'll do it later." But later doesn't happen for several days—it only arrives when I can't stand the guilt anymore. Then I'm motivated to get back on the path toward completing my goal. But look at the time I've wasted.
3. *Anxiety.* Ask yourself what you're afraid of should you accomplish your goal. At the root of most life issues is fear. When we give fear a name, we can better resolve what's holding us back from healthy change. Look

back at square 2 (self-sabotage). Ask what would happen if you stopped the self-sabotage. Do you now see a more direct path to achieving your goal?

4. *What I know for sure.* You've listed your goal, analyzed all the ways you sabotage yourself, and challenged your anxiety; now write out what you know for sure about how you want to proceed from here. This can be an affirmation statement, a go-to statement, or a mantra that will feed your motivation, get you back on track, and keep you going. If your goal is to exercise, your self-sabotage is laziness, and your fear is of failing to be disciplined, what you know for sure may be, "I feel good after a workout," or your affirmation may be, "This is my time. I do this for myself one hour each day."

Notes

Chapter 3: Change Doesn't Happen Overnight
1. Arlene F. Harder, "The Developmental Stages of Erik Erikson," February 26, 2008, http://first5kern.org/wp-content/uploads/sites/21/2014/10/TheDevelopmentalStagesofErik.pdf (accessed July 20, 2016).

Chapter 4: Igniting the Spark Inside You
1. Tony Robbins, "Why We Do What We Do," TED Talk, February 2006, http://www.ted.com/talks/tony_robbins_asks_why_we_do_what_we_do#t-433492 (accessed July 20, 2016).

Chapter 6: Changing from the Inside Out
1. Horatio G. Spafford, "It Is Well with My Soul," hymn, 1873.

Chapter 7: Breaking the Beast Hidden Deep in a Habit
1. Corrie ten Boom, Goodreads, https://www.goodreads.com/quotes/26993-it-is-not-my-ability-but-my-response-to-god-s (accessed July 29, 2016).

Chapter 8: Reengineering Your Life—Exchanging Bad Habits for Good
1. Marcel Proust, Values.com, http://www.values.com/inspirational-quotes/6885-let-us-be-grateful-to-people-who-make-us-happy (accessed July 29, 2016).

Chapter 9: Dealing with Unexpected Change
1. Victor Frankl, Goodreads, https://www.goodreads.com/quotes/52939-when-we-are-no-longer-able-to-change-a-situation (accessed July 29, 2016).

Chapter 10: Know Yourself, Find Your Purpose
1. Jeff Triplette, e-mail message to author, 2009, used by permission.
2. Zig Ziglar, Values.com, http://www.values.com/inspirational-quotes/4548-put-all-excuses-aside-and-remember-this-you (accessed July 29, 2016).

Chapter 12: Keeping a Healthy Frame of Mind
1. Voltaire, Goodreads, https://www.goodreads.com/quotes/37638-if-we-do-not-find-anything-very-pleasant-at-least (accessed July 29, 2016).

Chapter 14: Guarding Your Life in a World of Demands
1. Eugene L. Clark, "Nothing Is Impossible," hymn, 1966.

Chapter 16: Maintaining a Balanced Life
1. Hugh Sidey, izQuotes, http://izquotes.com/quote/297114 (accessed July 29, 2016).
2. Alexander Pope, Inspirational Words of Wisdom, http://www.wow4u.com/excuses/index.html (accessed July 29, 2016).
3. George Washington Carver, Goodreads, https://www.goodreads.com/quotes/339608-ninety-nine-percent-of-all-failures-come-from-people-who-have (accessed July 29, 2016).